Milwaukee County's
OAK LEAF TRAIL

Milwaukee County's
OAK LEAF TRAIL
A HISTORY

JILL ROTHENBUELER MAHER

Foreword by Amelia Kegel

Published by The History Press
Charleston, SC
www.historypress.com

Copyright © 2019 by Jill Rothenbueler Maher
All rights reserved

Front cover, top: Courtesy Burton Davis; left, author's collection; middle and lower right, Burton Davis. Back cover, top: Burton Davis; bottom, Eddee Daniel.

First published 2019

Manufactured in the United States

ISBN 9781467140683

Library of Congress Control Number: 2018966261

Notice: The information in this book is true and complete to the best of our knowledge. It is offered without guarantee on the part of the author or The History Press. The author and The History Press disclaim all liability in connection with the use of this book.

All rights reserved. No part of this book may be reproduced or transmitted in any form whatsoever without prior written permission from the publisher except in the case of brief quotations embodied in critical articles and reviews.

This is our Park by day or by night, everybody's fine front yard, enjoyed by so many in so many different ways.

—*Marjorie M. Bitker,* Milwaukee Magazine, *November 1968*

CONTENTS

Foreword, by Amelia Kegel   9
Acknowledgements   13
Introduction   15

PART I: BIRTH OF THE OAK LEAF   17
    Early Parks   19
    Velocipede Mania   21
    1890s   22
    1930s   25
    1950s   29
    1960s   29
    1970s   38
    76 Bike Trail Opening   43
    Security Concerns   46
    1980s   49
    Two Significant Improvements   53
    1990s   56
    Oak Leaf Trail Renaming   59
    2000s   61

Contents

Part II: Milwaukee River Line: Brown Deer, Kletzsch, Lincoln,
    Estabrook, Lake, McKinley and Veterans Parks   77
  Brown Deer Park   79
  Kletzsch Park   80
  Lincoln Park   81
  Estabrook Park   84
  Lake Park   90
  1972 U.S. Road Racing Championships   95
  Encroachment Concerns   97
  Waterfront Entities   98
  Nike Missile Site   100
  Short-Term Rentals   101

Part III: South Shore Line: Cupertino, South Shore, Bay View,
    Sheridan, Warnimont and Grant Parks   103
  Russell Avenue   104
  Hoan Bridge   106
  Ferry Options   113
  Bay View Park   120
  Sheridan Park   122
  Civilian Conservation Corps and Warnimont Park   126
  Cudahy Gun Club   127
  Warnimont Nike Missile Site   128
  Grant Park   129
  Grant Golfing   130
  South Milwaukee Yacht Club   134

"Meet Me on the Oak Leaf"—Song Lyrics by John Stano   137

Notes   139
Index   157
About the Author   159

FOREWORD

I feel very fortunate to have grown up in the Milwaukee area at a time when the Oak Leaf Trail was in place and ready to be enjoyed. Growing up with a dad who liked to bike, I feel especially lucky. Every weekend, he would wake me up early and ask me to go for a ride with him. We would go for jaunts around the neighborhood, take a back-road adventure to get lunch, but nothing sticks out in my memory quite as vividly as the first time he took me for a ride on the Oak Leaf. I was about ten years old, and I was absolutely amazed. I could not believe that there was a place where people could walk and ride in such peaceful bliss. Coasting along that section of the trail from Estabrook Park toward the lakefront downtown, I remember being very curious and somewhat confused. How had I never known this magical place existed? I remember asking my dad how this place came to be and remember how excited he was to share the details. Over the years, we explored many of the different segments together. Along the way, he explained how these systems were created. He made it very clear—trail systems like this only exist due to decades of planning and cooperation. It's the long game, he'd say, plant the seeds, and in a couple of decades, you might get lucky and get a trail. This insight has always stuck with me.

After years of taking the side roads in life, including riding three thousand miles across the country, working on organic farms and hugging the big trees of Canada, I find myself making roots back in Milwaukee. Since moving back, I've followed in my dad's footsteps in many ways. I was lucky enough to spend the better part of five years working alongside him and continuing

Foreword

our tradition of going for rides together. After his passing in 2017, my siblings and I have made a pact to keep his legacy alive and make him and our mom proud. My brother Noel and I are now the owners of Wheel & Sprocket, the chain of bike shops our dad, Chris Kegel, spent his lifetime cultivating. The bike shop started small in Hales Corners, Wisconsin, and grew throughout the years with the commitment to make our communities better places for bikes. Early on in his career, our dad realized that selling bikes was only a part of the equation to make communities bike friendly. The more important and more difficult task at hand was to create places for people to enjoy. Safe and connected bike trail systems are those perfect places to learn to fall in love with riding, nature and your local surroundings. Dad knew bike paths, parkways and trails could be used as an umbrella for many great outdoor recreational activities to thrive.

Like him, I now also volunteer my time on the Milwaukee County Trail Council in an effort to continue trail improvements for future generations to enjoy. It is a humbling experience to see how many dedicated individuals, organizations and businesses work together to conserve and enhance our public resources for many user groups. Though it is not always easy, I am proud to witness firsthand the planning that goes into the maintenance and development of these important places. Patience and persistence coupled with passion and cooperation build great trail systems. Though it may take decades, these public spaces, like the Milwaukee County Parks' Oak Leaf Trail, are integral to the health of our communities. We are all stewards of our natural surroundings, and planting seeds now help ensures continual success.

There is no doubt in my mind that the strong adoration I have for nature and our city stemmed from those childhood days when I fell in love with the Oak Leaf Trail. As a kid, I just thought we were having fun and getting to spend time together. In hindsight, I realize the lessons I learned from my dad while riding the trail from an early age helped shape the person I have become. But not everyone gets so lucky. Today, I make a point to take friends and visitors on the trail whenever possible. While I always enjoy hiking, biking the trail just lets you travel the distance to truly appreciate how special these 125 miles of trail really are. One of my favorite sections is the Root River Parkway between Whitnall Park and the sports complex. Following the parkway over boardwalks and through meadow-lined rivers has a special way of putting a smile on people's faces. Try taking a kid or a friend on the trail for the first time and watch their eyes light up.

Foreword

The Oak Leaf Trail is open 365 days per year, and at the end of the day, it is one of the best places to be able to reset, reflect and find solace. It is also one of the best places to come together and create those simple moments with friends and loved ones you will never forget. No matter which segment you choose, remember to take a second to thank those people and organizations that helped lay the trail before us. I hope this book will help deepen your appreciation for the history behind our wonderful Oak Leaf Trail.

Enjoy, and happy trails!

—Amelia Kegel

ACKNOWLEDGEMENTS

My parents deserve huge thanks for raising me right and buying me my first bicycle. While I wasn't always eager to go hiking, biking or cross-country skiing, I'm glad they shared their love of nature with me and my sister. Throughout the concept, research, writing and revising phases, my husband and daughter and larger family cheered me on. (So did dozens of close friends and new acquaintances who routinely told me, "I love the Oak Leaf!")

John Rodrigue at The History Press was always encouraging and insightful. His guidance kept this book on track. Experts helped during my research phase, including Kevin Abing and Steve Schaffer at the Milwaukee County Historical Society; Milwaukee County Parks Department employees Guy Smith, Bill Waldron and Ramsey Radakovich; Wisconsin Department of Natural Resources employee Melissa Cook; Kathy Mulvey at the Bay View Historical Society; and Michelle Gibbs at the Cudahy Family Library. Barbara Ali and Laurie Muench helped with local parks information and contacts, and Scott Wilke generously provided additional contacts from the Milwaukee biking community. Kim Suhr at Red Oak Writing LLC and the Red Oak Thursday morning crew provided insightful feedback and encouragement.

I deeply appreciate the inspiring photographers, musicians and painters who shared their work, including Eddee Daniel, Burton Davis, Hal Koenig, John Stano and Jenna Stoll.

INTRODUCTION

Each experience on the asphalt is unique. A day will offer just the right conditions, the type where you don't even think about the temperature as you exert to get up a hill. You don't feel weather on your skin, you simply merge with the outdoors. The sun might be combined with just the right touch of cumulus clouds, and you wish painter John Constable could capture it.

The other trail users will be particularly friendly, calling "hello" as they pass. A friend that you didn't arrange to see will materialize and you'll pull off your sunglasses to see each other better. Stepping aside the trail will shift you from one stress-reliever, exercise, to its partner, good conversation. You'll quickly catch up along the side of the trail and promise to reconnect again soon. Perhaps you'll meet for a walk on the trail together in a few months and make the first footprints on new-fallen snow.

You'll see an animal you never glimpsed on the trail before, such as the eagle my husband saw along South Shore or the five deer I spotted. Maybe some delightful birds will pass by just to tease you a little. A coyote may turn up, looking a bit menacing. Geese may flock together and pass overhead as harbingers of autumn. Even if they aren't your favorite animal, the sound of their wings over your head will inspire you to appreciate the moment.

Your mind won't perseverate on the grocery list or the car repair; instead, it'll remain gloriously stuck on that same patch of asphalt that you're enjoying. But your thoughts won't be down on the pavement, they will soar

Introduction

and open to the wider world. The sense of comfort mixed with uniqueness will keep you coming back.

Down on the trail, you'll see that no year matches another. The wild raspberries might be particularly abundant, or a new route may open. A forty-year-old hits a new distance, or an elder learns to cut back and keep smiling. A child outgrows training wheels or starts to beat her mom up a hill. The asphalt remains stuck in its spot while you cross it.

As life evolves, it's always a good day on the Oak Leaf.

Part I

BIRTH OF THE OAK LEAF

When a jogger turns eastward and savors a pastel sunrise or a bicyclist hits the brakes and pauses to drink in the beautiful color of a fall day, they satisfy a deep impulse. People fulfill their spirit by looking at glorious natural displays such as the sun rising over Lake Michigan. Some feel they reach God through nature, others enjoy breathing deeply in oxygen-rich air, and many are seeking a great workout.

People have been active along the lakefront and other waterways for centuries. Members of the native tribes such as the Sauk and Menomonee walked routes like today's Kinnickinnic Avenue as part of their daily life. Native travelers' footsteps wore these trails down below the surface level. These walkers undoubtedly caught a lake breeze and occasionally turned to appreciate the huge body of fresh water that helped sustain them. Perhaps they noticed a flock of birds overhead and experienced an appreciative moment of awe while actually hearing the wind whistle through an overhead bird's wings. When Europeans settled in the area, some of these routes eventually became roads, and a small part of Kinnickinnic Avenue is now included in the Oak Leaf Trail.

As time passed, European immigrants took over, establishing white governments and businesses. The 1833 Treaty of Chicago, between Native Americans and white settlers, included the land we now call Wisconsin. The years progressed, and a winding chain of events led to the buildup of modern transportation options. Milwaukee County, the entity eventually responsible for the Oak Leaf Trail, got its start in 1835 when it formed out of the larger

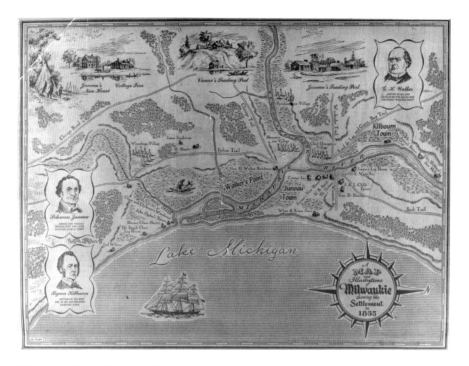

Walking trails established by Native Americans were clearly marked on this early map. European immigrants' houses were rare and individually depicted. Note the spelling of "Milwaukie River." *Milwaukee County Historical Society.*

Brown County. The county's early roads were treacherous and muddy. Local governments began building roads from oak planks, sometimes charging hefty tolls, which were worth paying because they significantly reduced travel time. Of course, these roads were carrying people driving teams of horses, not automobiles. It's interesting to note that the first transportation paths were built with oak, an eventual symbol of the county parks celebrated in the name of the recreation trail.

Through a meandering path, this county government would eventually create the route that became the Oak Leaf Trail. These leaders would create a route connecting large parks, some of which were on land donated or sold at a reduced price by business leaders and politicians. Their generosity combined with ambitious planning and intergovernmental cooperation—and even the cooperation of private companies. Leaders looking to create trails would eventually work with electric utility transfer companies and railroads, organizations whose business model requires long continuous stretches of land—just the type of parcels needed for an urban recreational trail. Like any product of the natural world, the trail's creation was not straight like a surveyor's line but meandering, following the natural order of things, with bursts of growth interspersed with periods of quiescence.

EARLY PARKS

Local parks developed beginning in the 1840s and operated through the 1910s, though they were quite different from what today's Milwaukeean envisions as a county park. Private owners ran them based on a business model requiring entry fees. One well-known park was the New Pabst Whitefish Resort, immediately north of today's Big Bay Park. Captain Frederick Pabst opened it in 1889, and it entertained crowds until 1914 with attractions like a Ferris wheel.[1] Later, many of these sites converted to the public parks enjoyed by today's population with upkeep and improvement funded by taxes and other revenue sources.

The city got serious about parks around 1889, and the legislature created a citizen committee. Then the idea of a park commission at the county level developed. About one hundred years later, an account in *Milwaukee* magazine describes the origin of the county park system and references Charles Whitnall:

> *The idea of a county park system was born in a schoolhouse. The story, as told later by Whitnall, was that several men arrived early at a lecture course one evening and got to chewing over problems of the day.*
>
> *One of them—it probably was Whitnall himself—lamented that "a city like Milwaukee should destroy the most effectual bits of the natural landscape," then later have to buy land for 10 times its original value to achieve "a tranquil environment."*
>
> *"Can't we still save some of it?" was the response.*
>
> *The conversation led to a move for creation of a county park commission. Col. [Charles] Estabrook, an assemblyman at the time and a former state attorney general, helped push a bill through the legislature in 1907 that created the commission.*
>
> *It was a good law. It specified that the seven member commission be non-partisan and nonsalaried. Members were to serve staggered seven year terms.*

Milwaukee County's Oak Leaf Trail

> *These wise provisions assured continuity and a selection of members based on their interest in parks and recreation, not because they had a political ax to grind or needed a pension.*[2]

Whitnall's concern about the destruction of the natural landscape may surprise a modern Milwaukeean. Trees fill today's parks, in stark contrast to prior destruction of the natural landscape. Abundance can devalue a resource, and popular opinion did not value trees. Farmers found them to be obstacles to their agriculture, and the whole city needed lumber and firewood for development. They resorted to clearcutting and made the surrounding area very barren in the late 1800s. As historian John Gurda has reported, the city's failure to preserve some trees was a civic embarrassment. Prior to this period of destruction, trees had thrived since the glaciers moved out and were once so commonplace that they were called "oppressively plentiful."[3]

County board chair C.T. Fisher appointed the commission Whitnall had advocated for, and these first members of the parks board were political leaders and company titans: Alfred Clas, Patrick Cudahy, James Currie, Emerson Hoyt, Alvin Kletzsch, William Lindsay and Charles Whitnall. A 1965 article points out that in its first fifty-eight years, the county park commission had only twenty-six members. For a time, the area had both a city park board and a county park commission. (The county park commission operated through 1981, when the County Board of Supervisors abolished it effective in 1982.)

The Milwaukee Board of Park Commissioners purchased land for several major parks from 1890 to 1907, and many are still in use today. Some land was donated, dating back to early founders: Solomon Juneau, Byron Kilbourn and George Walker all donated small tracts in the 1830s. Joseph Schlitz Brewing Company donated a large parcel along the river south of East Edgewood Avenue in 1940.[4] Patrick Cudahy later made significant contributions to parkland acquisition, including backing a loan for Grant Park.

Notable landscape architect Frederick Law Olmsted, who laid out famous parks like Central Park in New York and the Capitol grounds in Washington, D.C., planned Milwaukee's Lake, Riverside and Washington Parks. A carefully landscaped boulevard, Newberry, connected Riverside and Lake Parks.

Some of these nascent parks protected huge swaths of lakefront or riverfront property with gorgeous views. Instead of reserving these vistas only for the privileged, early planners set aside acres and acres for anyone to enter and savor. Beautiful sections of land along rivers leading to Lake Michigan became public property to enjoy and also alleviated flooding, because rising water would hit parkland before reaching homes or businesses. In addition, planners set aside huge inland parks to host countless picnics. Group sports like baseball, softball, golf and soccer and individual sports like bicycling and running had to gain popularity before they could become commonplace in parks.

Early on, jogging was not the ordinary recreational activity we consider it today. European immigrant adults did not commonly jog for exercise or to fulfill a hobby. The few athletes across the county who did pick up the sport did not immediately have organized races to join. The Boston Marathon changed all that. Running began to be considered a sport, at least for adult males, with the first Boston Marathon in 1897. It would grow over the years and become a premier American long-distance race along with the New York City Marathon. Milwaukee would not get its own marathon for many years, but the idea would eventually migrate westward.

Bicycling was as unusual a weekend activity as running. Bicycles were first thought of as unsafe oddities and gradually grew into a hobby of their own. Both bicycling and running were led by elite athletes who pioneered trends that the mainstream later adopted. European elites were the true trendsetters.

VELOCIPEDE MANIA

On a January day in 1869, Joshua G. Towne rode the first bicycle that Milwaukeeans had ever seen and made the newspaper. Wisconsin was then considered the West, and it was an early adopter in the region of an invention stemming from Europe and the East Coast.[5] Bicycling on wooden wheels became "velocipede mania," from a French term for "fast feet." Private rinks very quickly developed along with riding schools to help adults learn this new skill. Milwaukee resident C.D. Veazue opened a bicycle school at the site of an old skating rink where an auditorium later stood. Some people reported that those riding at night crashed into pedestrians and advocated for headlights and bells similar to ships.[6]

Experts performed tricks for paying customers and also taught new riders the basics. Trick rider Edith Shuler traveled from Chicago to provide a celebrity endorsement for Milwaukee's first bicycle rink. Some riders performed trick riding stunts similar to what skateboarders would do years

> ## Bike Jockeys Get New Equipment
>
> Innovation in this era included the jock strap. Domestic cyclists in this period were sometimes known as "bike jockeys," and they needed groin support while in the saddle. It was especially important over cobblestone roads. Responding to a request from the Boston Athletic Club's members, Charles Bennett of the Chicago sporting goods company Sharp and Smith invented it, and he used a knitted tight. He called it the "bike jockey strap."[7] In the 1920s, the Canadian company Guelph Elastic Hosiery made improvements to the design, including a hard cup for added protection. The brand name was Protex, and it was commonly known as the "jock strap," reflecting its bike jockey origins.

later. Like skateboarders, velocipede riders were sometimes considered a nuisance and faced a cultural backlash. The mania did not last, and the trend fizzled out in just a few months. It left behind a small but dedicated group of cyclists.

Some of these cyclists turned to high-wheel models, which were difficult to ride, and then safety models with broader appeal. The sport was primarily white and male. Competitive cyclists rode on banked tracks, sometimes using these tracks for multiple-day endurance races. Milwaukee held a six-day bicycle race that ended around 10:30 p.m. on August 14, 1880. The winning rider logged over six hundred miles and had come from New York. Only about 200 people watched the finish, so the ride was not profitable for its organizers.[8] (Decades later, local six-day rides would be well-attended, with the finish of a 1940s tandem ride drawing a full-capacity crowd of 3,400 to the auditorium.)

1890s

Bicycles evolved from dangerous oddities to safe, commonplace means of transportation and fun, and the area underwent another bicycle boom. Manufacturing towns with a labor pool skilled in small machine shops helped develop a bicycle industry. By 1900, the city of Milwaukee had at least seventy-five manufacturers, repair shops and bike dealers. The numbers had grown from two bicycle shops in 1888 and eleven in 1897.[9] Particularly when secondhand units and cheaper models became available, bicycling became a cultural force. It was less expensive than keeping a horse and helped increase a person's mobility.

Cyclists were faster than runners, of course, and crowds hadn't seen airplanes—or even cars or motorcycles. People of all walks of life enjoyed the hoopla surrounding large races, and bicycling was a hugely popular spectator sport.

> *It is difficult for us today, to reach back in our imagination to recreate the thrill and excitement of bicycle track racing between 1890 and 1910. Yet it was, nearly a hundred years ago, a hugely popular and surprisingly modern sport. In fact, among spectator sports in the United States during those two decades, it was certainly as popular as, if not more popular than, baseball, boxing or horse racing.*[10]

The competitive riders were primarily white males like Arthur Augustus Zimmerman, America's most famous rider. African American Marshall Walter "Major" Taylor set world records and achieved acclaim, but white racers and even officials conspired to keep him from winning races, and riders physically injured him. As described by Andrew Ritchie, travel in the South was particularly difficult for Taylor, because he was kept from hotels and denied service at restaurants. Lynching was disturbingly common, and Taylor was worried about training on the road and being attacked in what could be covered up as an accident.[11] The cyclist visited Wisconsin at least once—the *Green Bay Press Gazette* reported that he performed well in a League of American Wheelmen race in Green Bay and was heartily applauded for multiple victories.[12] Agents recruited him to race in France, where he was treated as a sports superstar and followed by supportive crowds.

Bicycles' popularity dissipated when cars became affordable and chased them out of popular use.

> *The boom stuttered to a halt in the early 1900s when the automobile became fashionable and practical. Thereafter, until about 1955, the bicycle was the vehicle for a small number of adults who rode them no matter what, through the up periods and down periods. And it became a rudimentary transportation method for children and this—for some 40 years—was the status of the bicycle.*[13]

Right: Marshall Walter "Major" Taylor was an early sports star whose dramatic career is the subject of several books. *New York Public Library Digital Collections.*

Below: Most early riders were white men, but sometimes women rode. Skirts gave way to pants or bloomers, allowing easier movement. This woman rides a motorized bike around 1917. *Library of Congress.*

Amid these national trends, Milwaukee County formed the park commission described earlier, and city and county parks coexisted. Charles Whitnall helped provide the concept of large parks for all citizens, referring to them as "lungs of the people." Whitnall would eventually be considered the father of the Milwaukee County park system and believed that green space should be available to everyone. After other careers, he spent forty years as Milwaukee's chief planner and was also on the city's public land commission and county's park commission.[14] He created a

Bicycles went through periods of innovation. These riders display a variety of styles, with the middle bike most recognizable by a current rider. *Library of Congress.*

master plan for the county in 1923 that largely has borne out, providing green spaces that bicycle riders would later enjoy. The huge Whitnall Park, originally called Hales Corners Park, was later named in his honor and eventually became a common starting point for enjoying the Oak Leaf Trail.

1930s

Whitnall's master plan focused on the water and considered the rivers, creeks and lakeshore. In a 1931 interview, he called the valley "the proper unit in the development of any territory." He hoped that no one would be more than a few blocks from a park. In general, his vision became reality over the decades, with Milwaukee County's more than 150 parks and 11 parkways (though many feel today's parks need more budget dollars to maintain their appeal). Parkways in particular would become an important part of future routes and would be enjoyed by decades of future riders who never knew they benefitted from Whitnall's vision and advocacy.

Bicycling was no longer eccentric yet still not commonplace, and recreational running was not on the radar. Harold "Zip" Morgan worked as the city's director of municipal athletics for forty-two years.[15] He was also vice president of the League of American Wheelmen and founder of the Wisconsin Council American Youth Hostel and combined those two interests by running two-day tours with an overnight stay at the Wauwatosa Youth Hostel. He worked with the Optimist Club and the Milwaukee County Park Commission to route riders through parkways and good roads around the county periphery. It was sometimes called the "Bicycle Tour of Milwaukee" and provided the foundation for future routes, including the Milwaukee 64, Milwaukee 76 and Oak Leaf Trail. His name would live in local bike lore history when, decades later, the "Zip" Line between Estabrook and Brown Deer Parks was named in his honor.

Political leaders recognized the inefficiency of having both city and county governments and proposed total consolidation. The state allowed only certain functions to consolidate, including parks. As of January 1, 1937, all city parks became owned and operated by the county. City of Milwaukee parks were not exactly extinct forever but became only side notes. For example, Zillman Park, at 2168 South Kinnickinnic Avenue in Milwaukee's Bay View neighborhood, is a small modern-day city park. In the same neighborhood, the Beulah Brinton Community Center, at 2555 South Bay Street, offers activities on greenspace that many would consider a park. It's operated by Milwaukee Recreation, which is part of Milwaukee Public Schools.

True to socialist ideals, nobody ever paid to enter a Milwaukee County park. Extra fees did apply for amenities like golf and swimming pools, but parks remained open and free to all who wanted to enter. This differs from the philosophy of nearby areas such as Waukesha County, which would eventually develop parks and collect entry fees to them. This approach also differs from the state of Wisconsin's park entry fees and trail passes on some state bike routes.

The city parks board ceased existence in 1937 with the merger of city and county parks. Citizen input was handled solely by the county park commission.

Local athletes gained some notoriety. Rider Ray Keller was a professional cyclist throughout the Midwest and some Canadian cities from 1934 until about 1940. A *Milwaukee Journal* article identifies him as an Allis-Chalmers employee in the 1960s residing at 5312 North Sixty-Second Street. He rode six-day races and also sprints.

> ### Victory bicycles help the war effort
>
> During World War II, the country focused on war production and getting the workforce to factories. Production of nonessential goods had to be curbed for the greater good, and the federal government froze bicycle sales. In December 1941, the Office of Production Management and leading bicycle manufacturing companies gathered to develop specifications for a stripped-down but very usable "Victory bicycle." This name echoed certain civilian efforts to help the war cause like Victory gardens.
>
> The Victory bicycle's features were finalized in March 1942.[16] The bike was:
>
> - Lightweight, eliminating about one third of the weight of prewar styles and maxing out at thirty-one pounds
> - Constructed of steel with no parts from precious copper or nickel
> - Free of accessories like a chain guard, luggage rack and bell
>
> Not just anybody could get one of the 750,000 bikes made each year. They went to adults who were employed, contributing to the war effort or contributing to public welfare with a compelling reason such as lack of public transportation, a heavy walking burden or a delivery service role. Within a month, the federal government further restricted eligibility to people like medical personnel, firefighters, police officers, construction workers and others. Some companies owned fleets of bicycles to help their workforce get to and from work and for on-the-job practicality such as meter reading.

Then widespread poverty hit in the Depression years. Despite the tough budgetary climate, local leaders like Dan Hoan advocated for continued spending on parks. As mayor, he was nationally recognized for good government, and he helped elevate the park system to one of the country's best.

Local Mel Welsh remembers buying a used bicycle for five dollars, which seemed more efficient than the ten-cent trolley fare to and from work. Some folks just didn't have the dime to afford the trolley. Mass transit costs plus gasoline rationing got workers accustomed to commuting via bicycle. Welsh recalls that Zip Morgan "started the bike trails because people had to have coupons for gasoline. His office was Thirty-Fifth and Clybourn [Streets]. Rationing was here, and Zip suggested that people use these bike trails to go to work. You might as well ride your bike and save your gasoline for Saturday and Sunday. That was the first time we really knew about bike trails."[17]

As the country emerged from World War II, locals gained a venue for the type of riding called "track cycling." Brown Deer Park hosted Olympic tryouts on a banked oval bicycle track with bleacher seating in 1948.[18] The track lacked lighting and a restroom for attendees but was nevertheless the site of the Olympic team selection. A Brown Deer rider went on to be one of the first people to speak publicly about bicycling trails in the parks.

Russell Kurtz, general superintendent in charge of park maintenance and operation, used to ride at Brown Deer Park with friend Del Lamb (an Olympic speed skater). Kurtz is quoted in a magazine article talking about improvements to the parks: " 'Another thing is more bicycle paths,' said Kurtz, visibly dreaming of fresh mornings spent spinning along on a

Stripped-down Victory bicycles helped the war effort. Pictured in Washington, D.C., are Leon Henderson, administrator of the Office of Price Administration, and Betty Barrett, an Office of Production Management stenographer. *Library of Congress.*

12 speed Schwinn lightweight. 'We have been traffic counting the less used walking paths and may turn some of them over to cyclists.' "[19]

1950s

From the 1950s through 1970s, the county expanded its park offerings with major projects such as the Milwaukee County Zoo, the Mitchell Park Conservatory (commonly known today as the "Domes") and the Milwaukee War Memorial Center. Local biking and running trails would one day pass near these landmarks. Amateur clubs also expanded, and Brian Murphy spearheaded the formation of the Milwaukee Track Club. In future years, this club would hold races and eventually become the Badgerland Striders, remaining an important part of the local scene. Groups like this helped build participation in running and created part of the demand for off-road running trails. Milwaukee hit the national running scene by winning a bid to hold the U.S. Track and Field Federation (USTFF) National Ten-Mile Championship in 1961 near Bradford Beach on land that later became the Milwaukee 76 and then the Oak Leaf Trail. The event was repeated in the same location for many years until it moved to Cudahy in 1971. The event added the USTFF National Championship for women on a three-mile route. It eventually became the Cudahy Classic, Wisconsin's oldest race.

As groups formed more infrastructure to help support increased interest in the running, contractors dug into the ground for the area's first freeway system. (Refer to Part 3 for more information about the controversial freeway.) The Milwaukee area had moved far beyond some wooden plank roads to much more sophisticated transportation options.

1960s

The 1960s brought a lot of change to the area, including construction of a first-class zoo and controversy over construction of the area's first freeway. Sports fans were concerned about the Milwaukee Braves leaving town. Cultural changes swept through the whole country. Bicycling and running got noticed. Surprisingly, a piece of legislation became a funding source that helped put significant dollars into outdoor projects and helped provide venues for these newly popular activities. The funding helped local governments build trails and undertake other projects. Congress established the Land and Water Conservation Fund (LAWCON) in 1964. It invested earnings from offshore oil and gas leasing into state and federal funds to help safeguard natural areas (including water resources) and provide recreation. Most people who enjoy outdoor recreation would be surprised to learn that some of their favorite amenities were funded in part by offshore oil and gas leases. The fund was initially established for a twenty-five-year period, then it was extended for another twenty-five years, and it was temporarily extended again for three years ending in September 2018. The county parks were able to obtain funding from this system to help create the Milwaukee 76. The funding was often a fifty-fifty split, significantly augmenting local funds with this larger pool of dollars. It may also have created a sense of urgency, because state and county politicians could take advantage of the opportunity to share the funding burden—the concept was "use it now or you may lose it."

In 1974, the general manager of the park commission requested permission from the county board to implement an application for LAWCON funds for the development of the South Lakefront and Milwaukee River bike trails. This included "The development of an 8' wide asphalt bicycle trail along the South Lakefront from South Shore Park to Grant Park, and the development of an 8' wide asphalt bicycle trail along the Milwaukee River Parkway from West Capitol Drive to West Good Hope Road."[20] The board of supervisors budgeted $116,000 for the South Lakefront trail and $86,000 for the Milwaukee River Trail and authorized the park commission to make the applications to the Wisconsin Department of Natural Resources.

LAWCON dollars helped create several segments of local bicycle trails. Funding sources like this helped spur high-level planning and intergovernmental coordination. In 1974, the county board got serious and said that Milwaukee County wanted to

1. *Urge the Park Commission to accelerate bikeway planning and development;*
2. *Urge the Park Commission to develop a recreational county wide bikeway plan;*
3. *Urge the Park Commission, Department of Public Works and Transportation, Intergovernmental Cooperative Council and the City of Milwaukee to develop a county wide bike land transportation plan for commuters;*

4. Urge the State Legislature and Department of Transportation to develop a statewide bikeway and bike lane plan to attract 70/30 federal participation through the Federal Highway Administration.

The county board seemed to want to put movers and shakers on alert that it was serious about biking. Politicians sent the resolution to County Executive John L. Doyne, Mayor Henry W. Maier, Intergovernmental Cooperative Council president Chester Krizek, County Park Commission manager Robert Mikula, Milwaukee County Department of Public Works director Henry Wildschut, Wisconsin Department of Transportation secretary Norman Clapp, speaker of the State Assembly Norman Anderson, president of the State Senate Martin Schreiber, clerk of the State Senate William Nugent and clerk of the State Assembly Thomas Hanson.[21]

Societal norms evolved quickly, and part of the new reality was increased roles for women. In the mid-1960s, the first woman joined the County Park Commission: Elizabeth Wyrick, who served from 1965 to 1971.[22] As women became more accepted in leadership roles, society also began to accept them as athletes. Female athletes banded together in 1968 to form the Badgerettes running club. This group competed in Amateur Athletic Union events, providing an athletic outlet for girls and women before female interscholastic sports were common. The athletes were fast: the Badgerettes won the National USTFF Cross Country Championships in 1971 and 1972.

Another new influence was interest in earth-friendly transportation and sport:

> *During the late 1960s there began a reawakening of adult interest in cycling as a non-polluting, non-congesting means of transportation and recreation. In 1970, nearly 5 million bicycles were manufactured in the United States, and an estimated 75 million riders shared 50 million bicycles, making cycling the nation's leading outdoor recreation.*[23]

Local bicyclists formed a tradition with a quasi-official annual bicycle ride beginning in the 1960s. Several local areas, such as Janesville (Rock 64) and Waukesha (Waukesha 64), held sixty-four-mile rides. Gerhardt Steinke organized the tour based on a route first established by Zip Morgan. It's tempting to think it started in 1964, but 1968 seems more accurate. A 1973 promotion includes a paragraph, titled "Story of the '64,' " that begins, "In 1968 under the event name MILWAUKEE 64 the first mass event taking in the entire route as a one-day tour was organized and conducted by Gerhardt (Gery) Steinke." The ride seems to have been fairly well attended, as the text continues, "Over the last six years well over a thousand bicyclists from throughout the mid-west have earned their MILWAUKEE 64 shoulder patch by completing at least once the '64' in Milwaukee." Riders were encouraged to stay at the Red Barn hostel, located on the route at 6750 West Loomis Road. The 1973 route started and ended at Lake Park Pavilion. The *Milwaukee Journal* printed the cue sheet, a page riders carried to know where to turn.

The 1973 route included segments that many modern Oak Leaf Trail riders would find familiar, though it seems to have included only four segments that were off road. These were in Bay View Park, Sheridan and Warnimont Parks, Greenfield Park and Lake Park. City streets and parkways brought riders through several major parks.

The Milwaukee 64 continued in 1974 and offered two different starting points, Wares Cycle bike shop off Seventy-Sixth Street as a west-side option or Lake Park as an east-side option. That year, the ride was scheduled to begin at 6:30 a.m., but a promotional page indicates that riders could start any time between 7:00 and 10:00 a.m. The ride was legitimate enough to have a finisher's badge and freebies like a cycling cap or water bottle, predating the swag bags with shirts and giveaways in future decades. Promotional materials make no reference to any charity benefit, which became commonplace for future rides. Organizers encouraged youth to join in as long as they were accompanied by a patient parent. A promotion makes the appeal to include young participants, at least boys:

> *Sixty-four miles is well within the grasp of any healthy child providing he is on good equipment and accompanied by a patient supportive parent. Perhaps the most important and most commonly neglected essential for an adult or child comfortably taking part in tours such as the* MILWAUKEE 64 *would be to have good equipment that rolls easily.*

Today's children are encouraged to exercise, but most would struggle to ride that distance in a single day.

The route was sometimes called the "Bicycle Tour of Milwaukee." It was marked with bike route signs, but these were often stolen. The 1973 cue sheet describes an attempt to stencil indications along the route instead of erecting more signs with this explanation: "Attempts to keep the 'Bike Route' signs on the route have been less than successful. An official who wishes to remain anonymous was quoted recently: 'We can well afford to put up sufficient signs to cover the route—but we can NOT afford to decorate all the uncounted bedrooms of sign collectors.' " The county board did authorize a $10,000 expenditure on the signs in 1974. The Bike Riders Advisory Board directed the expenditure.[24]

Local leaders noticed the increased interest in bicycling and took a significant step forward in the summer of 1964 by ordering a report in the next six months. At this time, any local riders could use the fairly extensive park roadways and bicycle trails, but several county supervisors saw an opportunity to do more. On June 23, 1964, Milwaukee County supervisors Joseph Greco, Marty Larsen, Ted Wedemeyer and Eugene Grobschmidt submitted a resolution:

> *WHEREAS, the increase in popularity of bicycling as a means of recreation has resulted in numerous children as well as adults using the local streets and sidewalks for such purpose at great risk to themselves, and*
> *WHEREAS, participation in bicycling should be encouraged, not only because it is a wholesome sport, but also because it is a means of furthering the national physical fitness program, and*
> *WHEREAS, the Milwaukee County Park Commission has recognized the need of providing facilities for the use of bicycling enthusiasts by designating existing roadways within the parks as bicycle trails, but such trails are not only inadequate to meet the increased popularity of the sport but do not provide the necessary protection against accidents and personal injuries, now, therefore,*
> *BE IT RESOLVED that the Milwaukee County Park Commission be and is hereby directed to make a study of the feasibility of extending and improving from a safety standpoint the existing facilities for bicycling within the county parks by building trails connecting several county parks, such as a trail along the lakefront connecting Grant, South Shore, Juneau, McKinley, Lake and Estabrook Parks.*
> *BE IT FURTHER RESOLVED, that the Park Commission file a report with the County Board on such study within six months together with recommendations for enlarging the existing facilities for bicyclists.*[25]

This marks one of the first official mentions of the trail that became the Milwaukee 76 and then the Oak Leaf. Though much of the rest of the vision came true, with a trail connecting the major parks the supervisors named, trail planners have never achieved a good connection along the lakefront between north and south. Here riders rely on city streets heavy with vehicle traffic, stoplights and cross-streets or patch together a route across some streets near the lake that frequently cross railroad tracks sunk in the pavement with a converted rail trail, which creates a nice ride but must be accessed from the busy First Street.

The County Park Commission, Division of Development, published a bicycling report in March 1966. At this time, county residents had registered 73,358 bicycles, and 38,734 were in the city of Milwaukee. The twenty-page report also contained two short appendices. The first page referenced President Lyndon Johnson, who was also quoted in the *Milwaukee Journal*: "The forgotten outdoorsmen of today are those who like to walk, hike or ride bicycles. For them we should have trails as well as highways. We can and should have an abundance of trails for walking, horseback riding and cycling."[26] The physician to President Eisenhower also advocated for bicycling as a way to help prevent heart disease and for other reasons. These activities were not yet booming but did become more commonplace. It noted that:

> *Much of the lands needed for the future parkway extension of Little Menomonee, Menomonee, Root River,* [and] *Oak Creek Parkways have been acquired, although it may be many years before the actual parkway drives are constructed. It is therefore recommended that a program of developing adequate bicycle trails which can also be used by hikers should be established through these acquired, but undeveloped properties.*

Charles Whitnall's plan to acquire land along the rivers became reality over the decades, as described in the report:

> *The parkway plan of conserving and utilizing those areas paralleling watercourses as storm water basins and constructing drives along them to connect the major parks has progressed steadily. Land ordinarily an eyesore have been beautified to the extent that many persons have purchased land and constructed homes bordering completed units. Winter and summer sport facilities are being provided where space allows.*[27]

The report detailed the values or benefits:

- Utilitarian—youth using bikes for paper routes, errands and deliveries and adults starting to commute for work or ride on a light shopping trip;

- Recreational—just plain fun, with American Youth Hostels, the Bicycle Institute of America and other organizations credited with "adding impetus to the surging interest in cycling as a wholesome and exciting recreational activity;"
- Physical fitness—with credit to the "sociological, psychological and physiological benefits of cycling."[28]

The report provided an overview of the county's efforts, including the Brown Deer Park velodrome, the 64 route and conducting bicycle safety classes with local police and service agencies.[29] It went on to make recommendations for county accommodation for biking and pointed out that the county's large parks are connected in many cases by the parkway system. "It is the recommendation of this report that bicycle trails should be established along these parkways utilizing the existing roads whenever the volume of vehicular traffic is not prohibitive."[30] In essence, the report recommended an expansion of the 64, a route that would eventually become the 76.

The county owned much of the necessary land, but that land sat undeveloped. This included the Little Menomonee, Menomonee, Root River and Oak Creek Parkways. The report indicated that creating trails would provide an outlet for athletes and also signal to the local municipalities that the county would do more with the land than just use it for flood control.[31] The estimated cost of parkway bike trails, assuming a five-foot-wide path with six-inch compacted road gravel and a bituminous seal coat, was $9,000 per mile. Bikeways, with a plant-mix bituminous concrete top course, would be much more expensive at $16,000 per mile.[32]

It may seem strange to a modern person, but in the 1960s, county ordinances prohibited riding bicycles with wheels over twenty inches in diameter upon the lawns, walks or foot trails in the parks and parkways. The report recommended this ordinance be amended.[33] The writers agreed with the rule in general but recommended exceptions to permit cycling on appropriate places, such as trails they recommended be established along Lincoln Memorial Drive in Lake-McKinley-Juneau Parks, in Grant-Warnimont-Sheridan Parks and Estabrook-Lincoln Parks. Improvement of the Brown Deer Bicycle Track (velodrome) was also recommended along with things like continuing to hold bike safety classes.

The report recommended specific routes that could provide "closed circuit, relatively short, recreational rides connecting with the major bike trails" The three were:

- Lake-McKinley-Juneau Parks along the west side of the busy Lincoln Memorial Drive. This general area would be the first to see an off-road, dedicated bike trail. The Chicago & Northwestern Railway Company was still using its nearby tracks, but planners had an eye on the land for conversion to a bike trail. They considered it temporary because of the Lake Freeway development they expected to be constructed in the late 1960s. (This section of freeway never got built due to citizen input.)
- Grant-Warnimont-Sheridan Parks from the Grant Park golf clubhouse heading north. A bridge was proposed to get cyclists over a ravine heading north to College Avenue. Planners assumed a high-rise building would require a short detour onto the road, after which the trail would resume off road, pass the military's Nike missile site and swing east through county-owned lands north to a connection with the recently extended park drive at Pulaski Avenue. This drive could carry riders to the end of Sheridan Park. This vision largely came to pass, without the detour past the private apartment building. Riders in this section at the end of College Avenue are brought close to the street but remain on an off-road path. The Grant-Warnimont-Sheridan section became one of the most beautiful portions of the trail, progressing on off-road paths through established trees with beautiful panoramic glimpses of Lake Michigan.
- Estabrook-Lincoln Parks along the banks of the Milwaukee River. Planners thought that minor grading of a little-used hiking trail could allow a cyclist to travel "in a total park environment without interference from vehicular traffic." The Port Washington Bridge would have to be modified to allow bicycle traffic. While this section took longer than the first two, and riders would travel high up rather than down along the banks, the general concept became a reality. Both Estabrook and Lincoln Parks have beautiful sections of trail, though riders must get through a busy street crossing separating them. Estabrook has a popular beer garden right next to the trail.

Wisconsin Electric Company (WEPCo) rights-of-way were considered a possible location for conversion to bikeway in the 1960s, but past experience made planners skeptical: "The biggest obstacle here is the fact that the Electric Company might be reluctant to permit this use because of the liabilities involved. Earlier negotiations with the Electric Company to utilize a portion of their right-of-way along Lincoln Creek Parkway for an archery range were stymied because of this liability problem."[34]

As described elsewhere in the book, the utility and the county were eventually able to reach agreements for several sections of bike trail to cross the utility's property. Riders in future decades would benefit from easements allowing access to the utility's land in multiple locations. The county paid for insurance to address the liability concern.

Across the United States, running for exercise and to get a natural, neurobiological lift—sometimes called a "runner's high"—became more prevalent. National magazine *Runner's World* began to cover the topic beginning in 1966. Bicycling got a big boost in Wisconsin when the Elroy–Sparta State Trail opened in 1965, the first rail-to-trail conversion in the county. The Rails-to-Trails Conservancy formed in 1986 and successfully advocated for converting railroad lines into recreational trails. Eventually,

---

WISCONSIN FINISHES FIRST

A few of Wisconsin's firsts and notables:

- First rail-trail conversion in the United States, which turned railroad right-of-way into bikeway (Elroy–Sparta State Trail, now part of four connected trails linking more than one hundred miles from Marshland to Reedsburg)
- Country's oldest operating velodrome for track-style cycling (in Kenosha)
- First bike ride to benefit the arts (became the United Performing Arts Fund [UPAF] Ride for the Arts)
- First public beer garden in the United States since the Prohibition era (located along the Oak Leaf Trail in Estabrook Park)
- Largest bike expo in the county (hosted each spring by Wheel & Sprocket bike stores)
- Longest-running women's golf club (started in 1934 and still operating in 2019 at Grant Park along the Oak Leaf Trail)

the Oak Leaf Trail would incorporate several stretches of converted former railroad rights-of-way. Some of these are straight sections with power lines nearby, such as the former North Shore Right of Way in Oak Creek. A heavily used section in today's Estabrook Park through Shorewood south into downtown was also converted.

1970s

Nationwide, the 1970s was the breakout decade that propelled both running and biking into common adult activities. Americans renewed their taste for healthy living in the 1970s, and Wisconsin senator Gaylord Nelson spearheaded the first Earth Day, signaling a renewed interest in conservation and all of the outdoors. The energy crisis led people to think twice about their reliance on cars. Decades after velocipede mania, another bicycle boom hit while a running boom also ignited. Both activities became commonplace.

- On the running front, Milwaukee had several organizations ready to accommodate runners who were inspired by Olympic champion Frank Shorter and informed by the bestselling book *The Complete Book of Running* by Jim Fixx.
- In 1974, California publishers launched two small American bicycling magazines, *Bicycling!* and *Bike World*. They kept the community linked and functioned as a hub of interest while providing race results, descriptions of long-distance tours, medical advice and reviews of new bicycles and components.[35]
- Bicycles got more accessible with lightweight derailleur-equipped models. This little invention helped ignite the bike boom by allowing riders to easily change their gear ratio by moving the chain, which made hills more manageable for riders. Derailleurs allowed ten speeds to become commonplace for adult bicycles.

Locally, a move foretold the abolishment of the park commission. In the 1970s, Milwaukee County adopted a cabinet form of government to comply with state law. This, combined with the county executive role established in 1959, put the commission in a more advisory role. As the Public Policy Forum reported:

> *This move did not bode well for the future of the Park Commission. A June 13, 1980* Milwaukee Journal *article reports the following statements by County Excutive O'Donnell, "A stronger county executive and a more politically active County Board have entered the picture. With a cabinet form of government, the Park Commission has been more advisory. Now O'Donnell, rather than the commission, appoints the head of the Department of Parks, Recreation and Culture."*[36]

For each park district in the county, a citizen advisory committee with seven residents of the district, appointed by the county executive, served staggered terms to get started and then three-year terms. The idea was to include more members elected by the people and receptive to the needs of the taxpayers.

In 1972, Milwaukee tried to host a marathon. Planners chose a month when the weather was unlikely to be cooperative for the first local marathon—December! The three-loop course at the lakefront took runners from Atwater Park to the present art museum and had to be shortened due to lousy weather. In future years, several Milwaukee marathons were offered, and locals would train for them along the Oak Leaf Trail. Their entry fees and pledges would raise money for local charities.

In the middle of the decade, county supervisors got serious about planning a race, but first they had to justify running, because the sport was still new:

> *WHEREAS, jogging has been found by the medical profession to be a beneficial and healthy mode of exercise; and*
> *WHEREAS, it would be beneficial to the citizens of Milwaukee County to be apprised of the health values in jogging; and*
> *WHEREAS, the "treks with the County Exec" were proven to be popular with the citizens of Milwaukee County; and*
> *WHEREAS, a County sponsored marathon race would publicize advantages of jogging; and*
> *WHEREAS, a marathon race would publicize Milwaukee County generally; now, therefore,*
> *BE IT RESOLVED, that a study be made to determine the feasibility of having the County sponsor a marathon race in the summer of 1978.*[37]

The county held a race, but it was a mini-marathon rather than full-blown marathon distance. County supervisors directed the general manager of the Milwaukee County Park Commission "to initiate a Milwaukee County sponsored mini-marathon on Nov 11, 1978 consisting of two races of 5,000 meters and 15,000 meters."[38] They figured the entry fee would sustain program costs and directed that excess money be deposited in a fund for future long-distance running events.

About five hundred participants enjoyed the competition and camaraderie of the Lakefront Discovery Run on November 11, 1978. Supervisors asked that the following year, the park commission schedule the event "at such a time that high school cross country runners may participate and not jeopardize their eligibility to participate in high school sports under WIAA and WISAA rules." Supervisors also urged collaboration with "groups such as the Badgerland Striders, the YMCA and YWCA, the *Milwaukee Journal* and Blue Cross of Wisconsin."[39]

By the middle of the 1980s, lakefront runs became so common that they were a nuisance to some. The problem was that a "considerable number of charity runs are held annually on the lakefront and county tenants who rent boat slips at the marina find it difficult to get to the parking lot due to barricades."[40] County board approval was required for runs in the area. In 1989, the events allowed to use Lincoln Memorial Drive were Al's Run and Walk; the Lakefront Discovery Run, organized by the Badgerland Striders; MAACC Fund Run; Milwaukee Wheelmen Bike Race; and Uecker's Ride for the Arts.[41] The circus parade—while not a race, run or ride—was a popular event included on the same list.

In 1973, Wisconsin governor Patrick Lucey approved Bill A-584, which authorized counties and municipalities to designate "bicycle ways." These could be a sidewalk or even a street or highway (or portion thereof). To help make recommendations for county consideration, the county board created the nine-member Milwaukee County Bike Riders Advisory Board. This included politicians, county employees and "four citizens exhibiting an interest in promoting bicycling as a form of recreating and insuring adequate and reasonable safety requirements consistent with stimulating interest in the sport." The chairman of this board was directed to appoint a seven-member Student Bicycle Advisory Council to provide "youth input in this growing enforcement and recreational problem which affects all ages of society and especially the young from a safety standpoint."[42]

Milwaukee County would need to cooperate with the City of Milwaukee to develop a meaningful plan. In April 1974, the Common Council of the City of Milwaukee adopted a resolution authorizing its commissioner of public works to designate bikeways on city streets. In June 1974, the county

> ### Companies Reach the Starting Line
>
> Two prominent local bicycle-related companies many people would recognize today were just getting to the starting line in the 1970s. Wheel & Sprocket began in 1973 in Hales Corners. By 2019, it had grown to four locations in the Milwaukee area, two in the Fox Valley and two more in the Chicago suburbs. Wisconsin-based Trek Bicycle opened in 1976, designing and manufacturing some of the bikes ridden on local streets and trails.[43] The company would diversify into multiple brand names for bikes, equipment and apparel and operate a nonprofit bike shop called DreamBikes in Madison and Milwaukee. The shop employs teenagers in disadvantaged neighborhoods and trains them to repair and sell donated used bikes.

designated its director of public works and general manager of the parks to coordinate with the city's commissioner of public works.[44] Thus a state action caused the city and county to work together, another example of intergovernmental coordination necessary to make a viable bike system in the area. They would create the '76 Milwaukee County Bike Tour as the overall plan.

At the last meeting of the year for 1975, humbly residing on one of the last of more than two thousand pages of proceedings for that year is the Milwaukee County Board of Supervisors resolution officially designating the 76 route:

> *WHEREAS, the Milwaukee County Board of Supervisors desires to encourage and promote bicycle riding as a means of transportation and recreation in Milwaukee County; and*
> *WHEREAS, Milwaukee County has established a "76 Bike Tour Route" around the County, which route traverses parks and parkways of the Milwaukee County Park System and local arterial streets between the park segments; and*
> *WHEREAS, the Congress of the United States has recognized the importance of bicycle travel and has included special provisions pertaining to this mode in the Federal Aid Highway Act of 1973; and*
> *WHEREAS, bicycle facilities may be constructed on Federal Aid System Highways with Federal participation in the cost thereof provided;*

The facility will not impair the safety of the motorist, bicyclist, or pedestrian;
The facility will form a segment located and designed pursuant to an overall plan;
A public agency has formally agreed to:
Operate and maintain the facility;
Ban all motorized vehicles other than maintenance vehicles, and when snow conditions and local regulations permit, snowmobiles.
It is reasonably expected that the facility will have sufficient use in relation to cost to justify its construction and maintenance; and
WHEREAS Milwaukee County desires to seek Federal Aid Highway fund participation in the development of its bicycle facilities; now, therefore,
BE IT RESOLVED that the "76 Milwaukee County Bike Tour" is established as the overall plan for Milwaukee County sponsored bicycle facility development; and
BE IT FURTHER RESOLVED, that Milwaukee County will operate and maintain facilities constructed as part of that plan utilizing Federal Aid Highway Funds, banning therefrom motorized vehicles except snowmobiles where snowmobiles are permitted by local regulations.
Fiscal Note:
It is anticipated that a total program cost of highway related bicycle facilities will be approximately $300,000. Under the present 70/30 Federal Aid financing formula, the net county share would be $90,000. The planning and construction activity would probably extend over a period of several years depending upon design requirements and the available flow of Federal Aid. A reasonable expectation of maximum single year county budget requirements for planning and construction would be $30,000. An annual appropriation for operation and maintenance will be required when facilities are completed.[45]

The trail would go on to become a beloved outdoor experience for many locals.

76 BIKE TRAIL OPENING

Local bicyclists got a truly official route with the Milwaukee 76 opening in the spring of 1976. It was occasionally called the '76 Bike Tour or "76" Bike Trail with slightly different punctuation. Whatever the name, red, white and blue signs marked the route. The top section showed a white men's cruiser bike with a red background, the middle section displayed "76" in blue and the bottom section contained a blue background and white directional arrow. These signs designated that the route was specifically for bicycling. In future decades, the route would open to multiple uses beyond bicycling. The patriotic colors of the signs helped reinforce that the trail was opening in the country's bicentennial year.

Colorful, patriotic signs indicated the route when the Milwaukee 76 opened to celebrate the country's bicentennial. *Burton Davis.*

Installing signs along this length of trail with multiple jurisdictions was not a simple undertaking. Park planning staff coordinated the signing project with utility companies, the state and twelve local municipalities. Staff in the park commission sign shop fabricated the signs, and county park and highway personnel installed them.

Integrated with the signing project was a map of the trail that was distributed by local bicycle dealers as well as by the park information service. In 1990, the Milwaukee County Board of Supervisors authorized the director of parks to conduct striping at the off-road portions of the trail with "dangerous curves."[46] The white center line guided riders to keep to the right half and minimize collisions.

The paper continued to support the sport and published the 76 route on April 27, 1976, but with a flaw. The paper then printed a correction to the route on May 4, 1976, under the headline "Setting It Straight:"

> *A map in* The Milwaukee Journal *April 27 showed the Milwaukee "76" Bike Tour in the Menomonee and Little Menomonee River Parkways as being connected.*
>
> *The map should have shown that the trail leaves the Menomonee River Parkway at Congress St. and runs along Highway 100 until it reaches*

MILWAUKEE COUNTY'S OAK LEAF TRAIL

This Grant Park scene shows the striped center line, a safety feature of the trail added in 1990 at dangerous curves. *Milwaukee County Historical Society.*

> *Hampton Ave. where it meets the Little Menomonee Parkway. The map, provided by Milwaukee County, was inaccurate and should have shown that that part of the trail was under construction and will be completed by the end of summer.*[47]

The map displayed the area in question with a solid line indicating "existing bike trail" rather than a dotted line indicating "under construction." As the correction explained, the 76 wasn't entirely complete when it opened in spring but was scheduled for completion well before the end of the summer, when riders could still enjoy it before cold weather arrived.

One of the brains behind the 76 was county parks landscape architect Irving Heipel. He had worked on it for at least nine years. The *Journal* reported the cost in 1976 at $447,000 in an article that shared Heipel's view that the trail wasn't getting enough attention.[48] He shared that the sections along the lakefront, including sections detailed in Parts 2 and 3 of this book, were the most popular part of the trail system.

Heipel and county colleagues had to work with several municipalities, and all of them were cooperative except for some disagreements with the City of Oak Creek. The problem stemmed from the use of Drexel Avenue as an east–west connection. Paul Milewski, an assistant director of planning for Oak Creek, said in 1976 that the road was busy with two-way traffic, and his city's leaders felt a better route could have been selected. Drexel Avenue did not bear 76 signs, because the city did not grant permission to the county. Oak Creek sought financial assistance for a Drexel Avenue bikeway in 1986 that seems to have gone unfulfilled.[49] To this day, riding east or west along Drexel has been challenging for many riders, some of whom call it "the dreaded Drexel." A path along a portion of the north side of the avenue opened in 2015.[50]

The April 1976 *Journal* article included quotes from pleasure riders and commuters and pleasant rider photographs. The page one photograph included a boy and girl, both identified as being seventeen years old, and a young family in the background. As was customary in the 1970s, none of those photographed wore helmets, including children. It was a stark contrast with future years, when helmets became common and doctors routinely asked about helmet use during children's yearly health care appointments. In 1992, the American Automobile Association (AAA) requested the county adopt an ordinance requiring the use of helmets by riders age fourteen and under.[51] It appears this plea was unsuccessful.

Riders along the 76 glimpsed several of the major parks, and some riders completed the whole route in a day. Bill Schlichtholz of Fox Point took part in an impressive traditional ride back when the Oak Leaf was known as the Milwaukee 76. His crew was young and fit and could keep up a pretty good pace. The yearly ride started the way many ideas are born, while enjoying drinks with friends in a bar. Somebody thought it'd be good to ride the route together, and they settled on a date in October. They became called the Reindeer, for reasons Schlichtholz always found a little fuzzy. "It might have had to do with the idea of riders being like reindeer pulling a sleigh, I'm not really sure," he explains.

In the 1970s, five to twenty-five Reindeer did the entire seventy-six miles in a single day. As the years progressed, the group dropped a small loop within Whitnall Park but continued to complete nearly the whole trail. They also switched from October to August for warmer temperatures. The fun-loving but athletic group would meet early in the morning in Fox Point and ride down to Grant Park, where it would enjoy breakfast in the golf clubhouse. (The clubhouse has since ended its breakfast offering but has casual dining and snacks during golf season and a summertime Friday fish fry.) Stragglers who couldn't match the main group's pace came in within ten or fifteen minutes and fueled up. After breakfast, the sweat and fun continued, and the riders would eventually hit a bar for lunch and make it back to the organizer's home for a barbecue.

Some years, participants' wives joined in for the first portion. To prepare, the group left some cars with bike racks in Grant Park overnight, and there the group separated, the women enjoying shopping after their shorter ride. "Sometimes people would bring a friend or their kid along. Some of them thought it was great and kept coming, others didn't like it so much," said Schlichtholz. The organizer even commemorated the event with plaques and handed out a small piece indicating each year. Schlichtholz lost two of the years' small pieces; otherwise, he would have a full plaque, because he never missed a year.

Ambitious groups like the Reindeers could reference a colorful foldout map produced in 1982 by a brewery or more plain sheets produced by the *Journal*. The trail provided a picturesque way to partake in the booming trend of recreational bicycling. Some commuters also relied on the trail, either year-round or on ice-free days, to get to work. The trail brought revenue to the area by attracting riders from outside the county who spent money at restaurants and patronized bicycle shops.

SECURITY CONCERNS

Unfortunately, security concerns also developed in the 1970s, with serious events in the parks as described by the Milwaukee County Board of Supervisors:

> *WHEREAS, events in recent years have demonstrated that vandalism, gang fights, rowdyism, criminal damage to property, assaults, battery, sex molestation and numerous acts of malicious, violent or aggressive nature often coupled even with other criminal conduct or acts have occurred through the Milwaukee County Park System, and*
> *WHEREAS, the situation cannot be tolerated; allowed to nourish or even accelerate if the citizenry of Milwaukee County are to continue to enjoy the best recreational, cultural and esthetic values in the entire country as represented by the Milwaukee County Park System.[52]*

These concerns led to greater reliance and authority for the county sheriff to handle parks, similar to the way Milwaukee County handles highway security. In addition to matching the highway approach, another part of the rationale was that the parks included thirteen thousand acres across the county. Sheriff Michael S. Wolke requested an additional twenty men to staff four deputy positions for the traffic bureau, including parking lots within the parks, in the summer of 1974. In typical Milwaukee fashion, the approach divided the north and south sides and planned two for each. The county board directed the sheriff to develop an auxiliary force composed of volunteers for use in the parks.[53]

People were truly scared to use the parks:

> *While it may appear to be logical to have all police functions under one head and all park functions under another, the fact of increasing public fears about even walking through the parks would seem to cast doubt on the wisdom of leaving them unguarded by officers who know every by-path of their domain. The proper use of Lake Park ravines is only one example of park landscape which should be carefully maintained but which will need patrol personnel familiar with the park and all its walkways.*[54]

Problems continued and even escalated. In an unusual show of solidarity, twenty county supervisors (all those in attendance) cosponsored a resolution. The disturbing resolution cites the brutal murder and rape of an eighteen-year-old girl along the Little Menomonee River in the vicinity of West Silver Spring Drive and, within the week, another savage rape of a young female in Kletzsch Park, which is along the Milwaukee River in Glendale. The sheriff of Milwaukee County was requested to offer a reward of $1,000 for useful information in each of the two cases. County officials intended this public reward to establish a precedent for future rewards in the event of similar "atrocious and barbarous acts" committed on county park property.[55] A woman was sexually assaulted in 1979 while jogging along a bike path in Shorewood.[56]

Criminal behavior like muggings and thefts flared up in 1979 in Lincoln Creek Parkway. After discussion with community members, officials adjusted the closing time for Lincoln Creek Parkway from Thirty-Fifth and Congress Streets to Sixtieth Street and Hampton Avenue from midnight to 10:00 p.m. (Eventually, all parks would close at 10:00 p.m.) The village of Greendale had problems with "vandalism, boisterous conduct and immoral actions" in the Root River Parkway.[57] An editorial in the *Milwaukee Journal* called for bicycle-mounted police patrolling the trails and increased squad car patrols nearby.[58]

Security concerns would flare up over the coming years. In 1982, during tough budget years, a request of $200,000 for overtime hours for patrol of the bike trails failed to get adopted.[59] The county board considered posting signs with emergency telephone numbers and noted that crimes "may possibly be reduced if bike riders and hikers were encouraged to go out in groups." It authorized the parks department and sheriff to work on suggestions and share them with the Milwaukee County Crime Prevention Commission for input.[60] The report was submitted in April 1983.[61]

Then, two women were sexually assaulted along the bicycle path in 1984. In a rash of July attacks, three more were attacked for a total of five on the northern end of the seventy-seven-mile trail between July 12 and July 27, 1984. In response, crews cleared and cut back brush along a one-mile stretch between the Lafayette Street Bridge and the Juneau Park lagoon

Sidewalks Are Not Safer

Adults new to riding often head for the sidewalk for the perceived safety. In reality, the danger of vehicles pulling out of alleys or driveways and the likelihood of striking a pedestrian make sidewalk riding dangerous. The city of Milwaukee has designated rules about riding on sidewalks which generally prohibit this for adults not on designated paths like the Hank Aaron and Beerline, crossing certain bridges and other reasonable exceptions.

> *City of Milwaukee 102-7. Bicycle Regulations. 1. RIDING ON PUBLIC WAYS. No bicycle shall be operated upon any public sidewalk, any pedestrian path in the public parks, or upon any public school grounds or public playgrounds. This subsection shall not apply to bicycles when operated on school grounds or playgrounds when officially sanctioned functions are in progress; bicycles operated by police officers in the necessary discharge of their official duties; or to sidewalks or sidewalk areas designated by the common council and identified by signs or other clear markings as a bicycle way. Children less than 10 years of age who are supervised by an adult may ride on any sidewalk that does not abut a building. A further exception is made for any disabled person to permit riding upon any public sidewalk or playground while accompanied by a responsible adult. When operating a bicycle on a bicycle way every driver shall yield the right-of-way to any pedestrian and shall exercise due care and give an audible signal when passing a bicycle driver or pedestrian proceeding in the same direction.[62]*

along Lincoln Memorial Drive. The intent was to make the path more visible from the parkway and to eliminate hiding places for attackers.[63] News of the attacks spread quickly among the bicycling community and reached the public via media such as the *Journal Sentinel* newspaper.

Occasional attacks continued over the years. In 2011, a bicyclist was stabbed near the 2100 block of North Oakland Avenue after a struggle over a cellphone. Police later arrested a transient man in connection with this attack.[64]

1980s

Charities like the United Performing Arts Fund (UPAF) benefitted from the fitness boom, and the tradition of a bike ride across the Hoan Bridge leading south heading out of downtown Milwaukee began as the Arts Pedalers Ride.[65] In 1981, Blue Cross & Blue Shield United of Wisconsin sponsored a twenty-four-mile ride from Milwaukee across the Hoan Bridge to Racine to benefit the United Performing Arts Center and the Racine Arts Council. Riders registered a few blocks west at Zeidler Park to minimize the time the Hoan closed to vehicle traffic.[66] This location had the advantage of being across the street from the sponsor's headquarters on Michigan Avenue.

The ride was thought to be the first in the nation to benefit the arts. In 1982, legendary sportscaster Bob Uecker became involved, and the event was named Uecker's Ride for the Arts. During an August 25, 2018 Milwaukee Brewers baseball broadcast, he reminisced about leading the ride and joked that being active was difficult on a Sunday morning. He further joked that he only biked one and a half blocks before taking a right turn, kidding the listening public that he bailed on the ride a short way through it.

For weekend warriors and other amateur riders, the event was a spring kickoff. Its various routes ran alongside portions of the 76, and people trained on the trail in preparation for the ride. It would eventually become the well-known and well-attended UPAF Ride for the Arts, Sponsored by Miller Lite, with routes of varying distances from five miles to seventy. It was one of the nation's largest single-day rides and raised $9.5 million since its origin.[67]

One of the early event participants was Mel Welsh, who had extensive experience riding his bike to work until he became a letter carrier. He retired in 1976 and kept riding for fun. He remembers the early rides:

Milwaukee County's Oak Leaf Trail

Riders—at least those who make it up the long incline—enjoy the views from the Hoan Bridge during a charity ride. *Author's collection.*

> *When the Ride for the Arts started, they asked us to wear helmets, but nobody wore them. It started at Blue Cross Blue Shield. We went over the [Hoan] bridge down into Bay View and Grant Park to Racine, and busses brought us back. Half the people dropped out going over the bridge. Only about half of 'em got down to Racine.*

Another bike ride, called Bucks for Bikes or Bucks for Bikes–76 Trail Ride, began in 1981 with proceeds used for improvements of the 76 bike trail. Bikers could stop at four stations: Lincoln Park, Grant Park near the golf clubhouse, Root River Parkway near Whitnall Park Drive and Little Menomonee River Parkway, where the trail met West Silver Spring Drive. Riders were encouraged to collect tax-deductible donations for each mile they rode. Blue Cross & Blue Shield of Wisconsin and the Sierra Club's Kettle Moraine Group were among the organizers.[68] It lasted at least seven years, a respectable stretch but not as long as the UPAF ride.

Another long-standing Milwaukee-area fitness tradition also began in 1981, this time for runners. The Badgerland Striders started the Lakefront

Marathon in 1981. It was still going strong in 2018 and boasts that it is "Milwaukee's original marathon" and "the legendary race of Milwaukee." In 2018, the route started at Grafton High School and wound its way south, ending in Veterans Park near the Oak Leaf Trail.[69]

A power shift occurred in 1981, when the Milwaukee County Board of Supervisors decided that the Milwaukee County Park Commission with citizen members would dissolve the following year. The county board would oversee parks, especially the board's Committee on Parks, Recreation and Culture. Day-to-day operations, of course, were handled by staff in the County Department of Parks, Recreation and Culture. This was a significant change in the governance of the county park system, which in turn governed the Milwaukee 76.

The early 1980s suffered an economic downturn. Over the years, political support for spending on trails seemed to wax and wane, and of course, not all budget appropriations made it all the way through the process to become reality. A reflection of economic troubles was the 1982 study of transferring responsibility for maintenance of the approximately 144 miles of county trunk highways and county parkways, some of which were part of the 76, from the county's responsibility to the municipality in which the roadway is located. The Milwaukee County Board of Supervisors noted that "utilization of work crews for local services would increase efficiency and reduce costs."[70]

In 1982, Milwaukee County supervisor Penny Podell (of the Third District) introduced a resolution to direct the parks department to study "making the '76 bike tour a safer route for bike riders and hikers."[71] The choice of words indicates that hiking was commonplace along the route, even though it was still designated a bike trail.

Riders in the Waukesha suburbs also enjoyed biking, and neighboring Waukesha County developed a bicycle trail on WEPCo right-of-way. The right-of-way reached Milwaukee in Greenfield Park at South 124th Street. Waukesha contracted to construct a bridge over South 124th Street, and the 76 trail was only eight hundred feet away, so the Milwaukee County Conservation Corps made part of the connection, and the rest was completed through a donation by the Sierra Club's John Muir Chapter, Southeastern Wisconsin Group. In a demonstration of interorganizational cooperation, a nonprofit worked with county government to finish the project and make the route better for citizens. In a cooperation between a utility company and a government, WEPCo allowed the trail to cross its lands, similar to the agreement made when the trail crossed the former Lakeside Power Plant in

Saffron Invaders Irk Citizens

The trail snakes past occasional dandelion patches within the park system. In 1973, Supervisor Rudolph Pohl of the Twentieth District had a little fun with the topic of weeds in the parks:

> WHEREAS, the County Park Commission and the Sewerage Commission have under their jurisdiction extensive lands frequently bordering fine residential properties; and
> WHEREAS, these lands may contain infestations of "noxious weeds" such as Yellow Dock, Canadian Thistle, Wild Mustard, Wild Barley, and of course our perennial favorite, Dandelion; and
> WHEREAS, notwithstanding the apparent scarcity of Dandelions on the British Isles, most citizens of Milwaukee County do not prefer fields basked in yellow; and
> WHEREAS, the preparties as cited above frequently continue unattended, allowing harvests of Dandelion seeds that are left to scatter on the winds to adjoining properties; and
> WHEREAS, disregard of proper property maintenance is frequently in violation of municipal ordinances governing "noxious weeds,"; now, therefore,
> BE IT RESOLVED, that the Milwaukee County Board of Supervisors assembled here this day, May 31, 1973, does hereby enjoin and request of both the Park Commission and the Sewerage Commission to maintain their respective properties and freeways with regard to "noxious weeds", including Dandelion, in an effort to maintain good neighbor relations with the citizenry.[72]

In 1987, the supervisors again had a little fun while modifying the dandelion policy:

> WHEREAS, the yellow peril of dandelions promises to blanket Milwaukee County and overwhelm both lawns and beleaguered gardeners; and
> WHEREAS, this growth now threatens to turn into a veritable cotton field and spread its seed across our residential neighborhoods; and
> WHEREAS, the Parks Director, in conformance with least risk County Board policy, is attempting to avoid the use of herbicides and, therefore, cannot mount an effective offensive against these noxious invaders; and
> WHEREAS, this limit on response should not be interpreted to mean no response as Milwaukee County should utilize its most effective weapons in this battle; and
> WHEREAS, it is essential that we develop successful tactics in weeding out these saffron invaders and assist harried homeowners by maintaining a good neighbor policy throughout Milwaukee County; now, therefore,
> BE IT RESOLVED that the Parks Director be and is hereby directed to evaluate potential solutions to the problem caused in neighborhoods by dandelions from the County's parks, and to prevent the entire community from being inundated, to expeditiously and more intensively mow areas of dandelion growth adjacent to populous neighborhoods and employ other alternatives which are determined to be both practical and effective.[73]

St. Francis along the South Shore Corridor.[74] Some experienced bikers used this route to commute into downtown, and other riders used it to extend their weekend rides. (Some connected to the Glacial Drumlin Trail to get to Madison.) Maps sometimes marked the Milwaukee County–Waukesha County trail link with wording like "Connector to New Berlin Rec Trail."[75]

Another connection to the western suburbs developed in 1985, again with successful, multilayered, intergovernmental cooperation. The county extended the 76 along the Underwood Creek Parkway, which extends into the city of Brookfield, where it crosses Wisconsin Department of Transportation and Milwaukee Railroad lands. The Milwaukee County Board of Supervisors cooperated with its own department of parks, recreation and culture; the City of New Berlin and Waukesha County; the Wisconsin Department of Transportation; and the Milwaukee Railroad. This successful cooperation extended the 76 trail to enhance riding in southeastern Wisconsin. Some maps indicate this link with "Connection to the Brookfield Greenway Trail."[76]

TWO SIGNIFICANT IMPROVEMENTS

The mid-1980s were a relatively quiet time for trail development, but two significant changes took place: the east–west segment was added and the Root River Parkway area was improved. The trail looked like a big oval, and that oval was about to get a horizontal addition—the east–west segment. This portion was sometimes called the "76 E-W" segment in official documents.

> *WHEREAS, the Department identified and evaluated a number of alternative routes for such a bike trail addition and narrowed in on two main alternatives: one in the Doyne Park/County Stadium/Zablocki VA Center/43rd Street Corridor (Alternative A), and the other in the Honey Creek Parkway/South 84th Street/Kinnickinnic River Parkway (Alternative B); and*
>
> *WHEREAS, traffic considerations, current pavement conditions and an immediate construction program mitigate against the South 43rd Street Corridor; and*
>
> *WHEREAS, traffic engineering, public works and administrative officials in the municipalities in which the proposed bike trail extends have no objections to the Alternative B route.[77]*

The expenditure was relatively modest, just $4,000 for the construction of two curb breaks and the installation of fifty signs.

The second big 1980s improvement came after county supervisors banded together to propose funding for a portion of the trail where residents had pointed out dangers.

> *WHEREAS, a number of County Board Supervisors have received reports from residents of Milwaukee County who use the '76 Bike Trail pointing out the dangers that exist on the Bike Trail when it moves away from the Root River Parkway at South 112th and 116th Streets and goes onto arterial streets from Morgan to Layton Avenue, and*
>
> *WHEREAS, in 1975, an alternative path was developed and recommended by the Parks Department that would alleviate the danger and provide a safe connection through parkland along the Root River Parkway at an estimated cost of $180,000, but has been repeatedly deferred due to higher priority projects....*
>
> *County Board of Supervisors do hereby recommend providing $180,000 in the Parks Department Capital Improvement Budget for the purpose of constructing an improved and safer Bike Trail section...along the Root River Parkway.*[78]

In 1988, the 76 East-West Trail opened on streets and parkways linking Wauwatosa with the trail at the lakefront in Milwaukee's Bay View neighborhood. It was sometimes called the "East-West Addition," and as the name indicates, it formed a belt across the middle of the loop. This area in West Allis and West Milwaukee created a horizontal connection that allowed some riders to take a shorter circular outing. They could ride just the northern loop or just the southern loop of the trail. Portions followed the Honey Creek and Kinnickinnic River Parkways and passed through Jackson and Humboldt Parks, adding a total of 14.3 miles to the 76 route. Just .6 miles of the East-West Trail was off road, with 7.6 on parkway drives and the remaining 6.1 on municipal streets. Around this time, the main 76 route was roughly split into thirds, with 26.8 off road, 23.5 on parkway drives and 25.2 on municipal streets.[79]

The Milwaukee Industrial Clinic held triathlons in the 1980s. Milwaukee hosted the U.S. Triathlon Association's 1986 Annual Board of Governors meeting and board of directors meeting July 25–27[80] and then bid for the national championship in 1987.

BICYCLING GETS NOTICED

On the national scene, events like these attracted more stateside attention to elite riding:

- American Greg LeMond placed third in 1984 in the esteemed historic twenty-one-stage Tour de France and won it all in 1986, the first win by an American. He went on to win in 1989 and 1990. He also won the Road Race World Championship in 1983 and 1989.
- Starting in 1980, the Ironman triathlon in Hawaii was televised on ABC's *Wide World of Sports*,[81] including some dramatic finishes with exhausted athletes crawling across the finish line. The race involved a 2.4-mile swim, a 112-mile bike race and a 26.2-mile run.
- In 1984, Los Angeles hosted the world's athletes for the Olympics. In bicycle racing, Connie Carpenter-Phinney and Rebecca Twigg finished first and second in the women's road race. Carpenter-Phinney, born in Madison, was a crossover from skating with phenomenal athletic ability, winning twelve U.S. cycling championships. Alexi Grewal took the gold in the men's road race, becoming the first American man to win an Olympic Gold Medal in road cycling. He just barely beat a Canadian rider in a showdown witnessed by thousands in person and many more via the media. Carpenter-Phinney and Grewal have remained the only American winners of the Olympic road race. American racers won medals in individual and team pursuit races as well. Olympic success was great publicity for the sport.
- Olympic organizers held the first women's Olympic marathon, and Joan Benoit (later Joan Benoit Samuelson) won with an unconventional strategy of pulling away from the pack early. She waved her white hat in celebration near her dominant finish and inspired more girls and women to run.

1990s

Several levels of government created plans in the 1990s. The City of Milwaukee developed one with the top goal of creating a new position of bicycle coordinator. Other goals were "striping bike lanes in our streets and changing the mentality of roadway design professionals to think about bicyclists, pedestrians and also motorists."[82] The Milwaukee County Department of Parks, Recreation and Culture formulated a master plan for bike trail expansion, and it was included in the larger report produced with the Southeastern Regional Planning Commission called *A Park and Open Space Plan for Milwaukee County*. It provided an update on the current trails and made recommendations for additional mileage:

> *Under the park and open space plan for Milwaukee County, it is recommended that about 131 miles of trails and bicycle routes be provided in the County....Of the 131 miles of trails and bicycle routes proposed to be provided in Milwaukee County, about 89 miles, or 68 percent, have been developed. It is recommended that these developed trails—which are located along the Lake Michigan shoreline; within the Kinnickinnic River, Lincoln Creek, Little Menomonee River, Menomonee River, Milwaukee River, Oak Creek, Root River, and Underwood Creek Parkways; and along Drexel avenue, Good Hope Road, and Bradley Road—be maintained.... The remaining 42 miles, or 32 percent, are recommended for development within the Little Menomonee River, Menomonee River Oak Creek, and Root River Parkways; and along Bradley Road, along Cleveland Avenue, in the lower Menomonee River Valley, and on the Hoan Bridge.*

At the federal level, reauthorization in 1990 of the Clean Air Act Amendment (CAAA) required that the Milwaukee area substantially reduce auto emissions over the next fifteen years or face federal sanctions. Converting drivers to bicyclists was a strategy to meet the requirements of the CAAA.[83]

In 1991, Congress enacted the Intermodal Surface Transportation Efficiency Act (ISTEA). This reauthorization of federally funded transportation programs included ten categories of transportation enhancements with some providing facilities for bikers and walkers—for example, funding for off-road trails used by bicycle commuters. Funding once dedicated to highways could be used in broader ways. This source provided a majority of the funding for several projects, such as the Northwest Bikeway from Good Hope Road to Bradley Road along the Little Menomonee River Parkway. On this project, the federal grant provided 80 percent of the $200,000 project with a 20 percent local contribution. (The county had applied to the Wisconsin Department of Natural Resources Stewardship Program grant for this section, but it was denied in 1992.)[84] In the mid-1990s, the county was able to spend significant money on trails. For example, the county planned to spend $1,109,000 in 1994 for its 20 percent share of three trails funded primarily by ISTEA dollars.[85] The county received ISTEA funding for at least one project nearly every year beginning in 1993. Some years, ISTEA funded as many as three local projects.

Supervisor Daniel Cupertino submitted an informative overview of the trails in 1993 in authorizing the County Department of Parks, Recreation and Culture to seek grant funding.

> *WHEREAS, these bike trails link urban, suburban, and rural areas in Milwaukee County providing access within the County and eventually to other counties as part of a national network; and*
>
> *WHEREAS, in addition to the recreation and physical fitness opportunities which bike trail corridors provide, they also provide vital ecological and environmental functions acting as natural buffers to separate commercial and residential areas, preserve trees and vegetation which purify air and filter water run-off flowing into river streams, and preserve local plants and animal life; and*
>
> *WHEREAS, by the year 2000, with more than 80 percent of the nation's population residing in urban areas, long-distance commuting will become more restrictive and close-to-home recreation opportunities will become more of a priority; and*
>
> *WHEREAS, the '76 Bike Trail is part of a new scenic drive along Lake Michigan which will appeal to tourists as well as residents and enhance the downtown area both visually and in terms of readily accessible recreation opportunities; now, therefore*
>
> *BE IT RESOLVED, that the Director of the Department of Parks, Recreation and Culture is hereby authorized and directed to pursue funding and submit applications for the improvement and upgrading of Milwaukee County bike trails, especially the '76 Bike Trail, from all available federal and State sources, especially those delineated under the Bicycle and Pedestrian Provisions of the Intermodal Surface Transportation Efficiency Act (ISTEA).*[86]

Congress replaced ISTEA with the Transportation Equity Act for the Twenty-First Century (TEA-21). The new program was structured on an 80 percent federal/20 percent local cost share and broadened how federal funds could be used for bicycle transportation and pedestrian walkways.[87] In another cooperative relationship, the East Side Business Improvement District came forward with money that allowed the county to request TEA-21 funds for an access ramp to the Oak Leaf Trail.[88] The grant application was successful, and the Brady Street bridge was eventually constructed at an estimated cost of $331,250, with 80 percent from the Wisconsin Department of Transportation, which administered TEA-21 funds at the state level. The county applied for additional funding through this source for the Hoyt Bikeway–Milwaukee Forestry segment and a conversion of former North Shore Railway right-of-way.[89]

Between 1993 and 2017, the county received over $20 million in funding from ISTEA, TEA-21 and the follow-on, the Safe, Accountable, Flexible, Efficient Transportation Equity Act: A Legacy for Users (SAFETEA-LU), which Congress passed in 2005.[90] Federal funding played a large part in making local biking trails a reality. State funding from the Wisconsin Department of Natural Resources Stewardship Program contributed over $3 million in the same time period.

Milwaukee mayor John Norquist had city staff create a task force that included public members and government representatives in 1991. They recommended that "the Mayor's Bicycle Task Force should be formally reconstituted into a permanent volunteer body, or Council, which includes public members and is staffed by the Bicycle Coordinator." Stephen Hiniker, environmental policy coordinator, chaired it, and seventeen other members participated.[91] Groups like this helped coalesce people who wanted to advocate for bicyclists (including on trails).

The City of Milwaukee did create the Bicycle Task Force via a common council resolution in May 1993. Ten years later, this group would become the Bicycle and Pedestrian Task Force, and its goal was to recommend ways to make Milwaukee a more bicycle- and pedestrian-friendly community. It was the formal means through which active citizen participation was provided to advise policymakers.[92] It consisted of eight citizen members, one safety professional, one representative of the Milwaukee Department of Public Works and one representative of the Milwaukee Department of City Development. The mayor appointed members, and the common council confirmed them.

OAK LEAF TRAIL RENAMING

In the summer of 1995, official documents started to refer to the trail as the "76 Multi-Use Trail." This acknowledged that it was open to walking and running as well as biking—and it was even available to dog walkers, a group that sometimes collides with bike riders. Unlike squirrels, who tend to scamper out of the way of a bicyclist, dogs and bike wheels sometimes collide. Eventually, people pushed jogging strollers and hid geocaches and even brought binoculars for birdwatching along the trail. The county recognized that twenty years had passed since the trail opened, and the route had expanded beyond seventy-six miles. In 1996, the County Parks Department renamed the 76 the Oak Leaf Trail. The oak leaf and acorn had long been associated with the parks, appearing on iconic brown signs at the "front door" to each park and in printed materials promoting the parks. Mike Rapp, a retired landscape architect for the parks, was involved with the renaming, and Susan Baldwin was the director of the department. Further details on the renaming are lost to history.[93]

The county purchased a bike trail easement from Stonewood Development Corporation for a portion of the former North Shore Railroad right-of-way between the city of Oak Creek's Greenlawn Park at 7628 South Howell Avenue and Rawson Avenue.[94] This created a useful southeast extension of the trail. At the southern portion of this section, an occasional horseback rider passes the more typical dog walker, hiker or bicyclist.

The county worked toward another improvement in Oak Creek and again cooperated with a utility by approving an easement from WEPCo for the construction, operation and maintenance of a bike trail across WEPCo property. County supervisors adopted the following:

> *WHEREAS, the Department of Parks, Recreation and Culture (DPRC) has in its adopted 1997 Capital Improvement Budget funding to construct a bike trail in Oak Creek Parkway from Pennsylvania Avenue on the east end to Drexel Avenue on the west end; and*
> *WHEREAS, this trail will be an extension of the County Oak Leaf Bike Trail system—the trail will consist of an off-road asphalt path which will pass through County park land and WEPCo property.*[95]

Another utility entered the picture, but this time it was a revenue-generating agreement. Fiber-optic networks had become a popular way to send information, and companies needed narrow, continuous stretches of

Horses are allowed on some sections of the trail, such as this area in Oak Creek. *Author's collection.*

land to build networks. Former railroad rights-of-way provided the perfect parcels, and Qwest build a network focused on this type of land throughout parts of the Midwest and West. The county entered an agreement that allowed Qwest Network Construction Services to install over ten miles of fiber-optic cable with about $57,000 annual income. The easement had a twenty-five-year term, potentially bringing in over $1,400,500.[96]

Intergovernmental disagreements occasionally flared up, for example over paying for an engineering study of the proposed Hoan Bridge Bicycle Trail. The Wisconsin Department of Transportation sought funding from the city for the 20 percent local portion of study funding. The rest was federally funded. Milwaukee County argued that "no other county or municipality in Wisconsin is required to contribute toward the cost of interstate highway projects;…Milwaukee County is the only county in the State which has ever had to contribute toward the cost of a state interstate highway project when in the 1960s and 1970s it paid half of the local share construction cost amounting to millions of dollars."[97] Another political squabble concerned easements for the Henry "Hank" Aaron State Trail when the county board sustained a veto on a resolution authorizing the corporate counsel to include sufficient lands for the trail in the property agreement for the new baseball stadium.[98]

Former Milwaukee mayor John Norquist spearheaded the trail's creation. The path that eventually became the Hank Aaron State Trail was a mere concept in the 1990s in a report by the Mayor's Bicycle Task Force. It stated, "An east/west route through the Menomonee River Valley along the Menomonee River, connecting the Lakefront to the Brewer Stadium area should be seriously considered. The potential for this route depends on a host of other local and state development issue in the Valley."[99]

2000s

Most locals call the trail the "Hank Aaron" and know that it's named after a retired professional baseball player who excelled at hitting home runs with the Milwaukee and Atlanta Braves and Milwaukee Brewers, becoming a hall-of-fame legend. The trail named after him opened in sections. In 2000, the Wisconsin Department of Natural Resources (DNR) developed the first segment of the trail, adjacent to the Miller Park baseball stadium, though it was only a third of a mile long. Next, the City of Milwaukee built a segment between Thirteenth Street and Twenty-Fifth Street. This small portion was funded through a Wisconsin Coastal Management Grant with a City of Milwaukee match. In 2006, this section directly connected to the Miller Park section when the city constructed an extension to Canal Street. Governor Jim Doyle, Milwaukee mayor Tom Barrett, Alderman Michael J. Murphy and Henry "Hank" Aaron joined other politicians and leaders in a special dedication ceremony marking the completion of one portion of the Hank Aaron State Trail.

In 2006, the DNR purchased five miles of railroad right-of-way to extend the Hank Aaron State Trail from Miller Park west to Underwood Creek Parkway using federal Congestion Mitigation and Air Quality Improvement program funding with a local match. This continuous segment of rail corridor almost doubled the length of the trail. It's generally an easy-to-ride, green section that does contain a few street crossings, though they are rare enough to provide a feeling of escape to nature. Several more miles linked in with a huge project in the Menomonee Valley, where an entirely new park was created. The Milwaukee Redevelopment Authority owned the Three Bridges Park land and granted the DNR an easement to operate the Hank

Aaron Trail.[100] (The entire park is jointly operated by the City of Milwaukee, DNR and Urban Ecology Center.)

In this area, trail users pass a former industrial area once spoiled with pollution from coal-burning factories. It became a uniquely beautiful ride along a valley. "But even as it winds through Milwaukee, around downtown, past the Harley-Davidson Museum…and beyond the Wisconsin state fairgrounds, it offers the allure of a quiet getaway. On the trail you may hear the chirp of crickets, or see herons wading in the river," wrote Jay Walljasper in *Rails-to-Trails* magazine.[101]

An extension of the city's RiverWalk was planned for the Menomonee River and was designed with a wide enough path to accommodate

A group gathers to ride to work along the Hank Aaron Trail, which connects to the Oak Leaf Trail. *Eddee Daniel.*

Birth of the Oak Leaf

Alderman Michael Murphy *(left)* and former baseball player Hank Aaron *(right)* at a ceremony marking the trail's opening. *City of Milwaukee Public Information Division.*

This walker enjoys fresh air on the Hank Aaron Trail despite cold temperatures. *Author's collection.*

bicyclists. Planners said it would connect and occasionally overlap with the Hank Aaron. Construction was set to begin in 2020 based on plans announced in 2017.[102]

The Lakeshore State Park opened downtown near Discovery World and the Henry W. Maier Festival Park (Summerfest Grounds) and included paths for walkers, bikers, runners and more. This allowed downtown workers another good lunchtime running route. In winter, it was one of the only local places where joggers could spot people nearby ice fishing in small structures called "shanties." In summer, they might see a dramatic three-masted wooden schooner, the sailing vessel *Denis Sullivan*, or wedding parties posed in formal wear for photographs with a backdrop of shortgrass prairies. This state park did not require admission stickers, and many people on the lakefront took advantage of it, using the segment alone or combining it with the nearby Oak Leaf Trail to continue north or south.

Eventually, the Hank Aaron's sections linked together to provide an east–west route extending from the western edge of the county east to the Lake Michigan shoreline. Achieving the vision of the Hank Aaron required cooperation of many groups, just like the Oak Leaf Trail's creation required various organizations to work together.

Coastal Zone Management Act of 1972

A Wisconsin Coastal Management Grant Program funded a portion of the Hank Aaron Trail in Lakeshore State Park. The Wisconsin Department of Administration (DOA) administers WCMP grants in collaboration with the Wisconsin Coastal Management Council (WCMC) and the Office for Coastal Management (OCM), U.S. Department of Commerce, through funding provided under the Coastal Zone Management Act of 1972. Grants fund projects like:

- Coastal wetland protection and habitat restoration
- Nonpoint source pollution control
- Coastal resource and community planning
- Great Lakes education
- Public access and historic preservation projects[103]

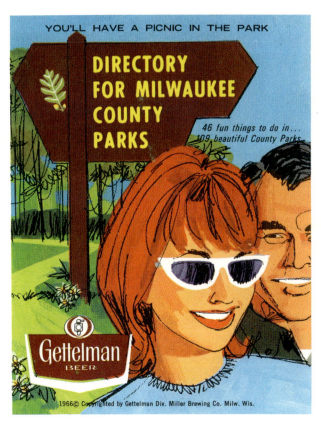

Above: This statue of Patrick Cudahy adorns Sheridan Park. The meatpacking company co-owner sold land at a discounted price for Sheridan Park and backed a loan for the purchase of Grant Park. *Gloria Rothenbueler.*

Left: The iconic brown signs bearing an oak leaf and acorn have long been a symbol for the county park system. *Milwaukee County Historical Society.*

Above: Rebuilding the trail and surrounding area in South Shore Park required heavy machinery. *Courtesy Bay View Historical Society/ Kathy Mulvey.*

Left: Locals hike or walk dogs through the solitude of Seminary Woods near the Oak Leaf Trail on the south shore. *Eddee Daniel.*

Many couples have met and deepened their relationships over a shared love for the outdoors and athletics, including along the Oak Leaf Trail. *Pixabay, Pexels.*

Nature lovers can experience a variety of wildlife along the trail, including herons near water. Glimpses of animals can help people escape the hectic pace of everyday life. *Eddee Daniel.*

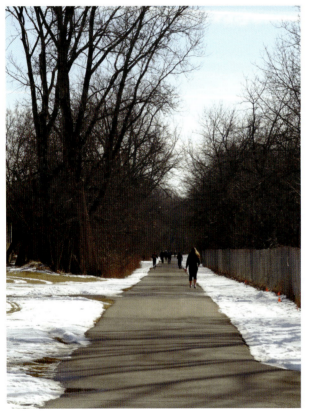

Above: Beautiful weather helps riders enjoy the trail. *Eddee Daniel.*

Left: Some ultra-straight sections of the Oak Leaf Trail are converted railroad rights-of-way. *Author's collection.*

Left: The Oak Leaf Trail relies on both railroad and electric utility rights-of-way. *Author's collection.*

Below: Benches along the trail, including this recently improved section at the South Shore Yacht Club in the Bay View neighborhood, provide great places to take in the scenery. While this is a commercially made bench, many others are produced by Boy Scouts. *Jenna Stoll Photography.*

The nonprofit Park People of Milwaukee County organized a way to help people learn more about the trail and see new parks. *Park People of Milwaukee County.*

Art and architecture loom large on the downtown Milwaukee portion of the Oak Leaf Trail. *Pixabay.*

This page: The UPAF Ride for the Arts, Sponsored by Miller Lite, allows bicyclists a thrilling, unique view. They see the lake to the east and downtown buildings to the west and north. *Both, author's collection.*

Top: This contemporary painting, *Late Afternoon Candles*, reflects the serene beauty along portions of the South Shore Corridor that hug the shoreline of Lake Michigan. *By Hal Koenig.*

Middle: At one time, most of the Milwaukee area was devoid of trees due to clearcutting. Now, trees are plentiful once again and oaks flourish near parts of the trail. *Painting,* Bay, *by Hal Koenig.*

Left: Moments alone on the trail can provide a deep stillness. *Painting,* Winter Skyline, *by Hal Koenig.*

Winter outings to the trail provide their own tranquility. In this scene, the straight route hints at the land's prior use as railroad right-of-way. *Author's collection.*

Nature provides lots of interesting scenes along the trail in winter. Here birds gather on ice near open water inside the Lake Michigan breakwater. *Author's collection.*

Sailboats provide a picturesque sight for people on the trail. *Pixabay.*

Group gatherings make workouts more fun. The Oak Leaf Trail can strengthen friendships by providing a cost-free way to enjoy time together. *Burton Davis.*

Lakefront views from the trail can be stunning. *Burton Davis.*

Landfill extended the parkland east of downtown and created new ways to enjoy the lakefront. *Burton Davis.*

Dogs are a common sight along the Oak Leaf Trail, even downtown. *Burton Davis.*

Parkland meets cityscape directly east of downtown. *Burton Davis*.

Established trees and a lagoon provide trail users a sense of tranquility, even near the popular Lincoln Memorial Drive. *Burton Davis*.

Left: People exercising downtown usually have lots of company along the Oak Leaf Trail. *Burton Davis*.

Below: The trail's South Shore Line can also get busy but often provides a glimpse of solitude. *Burton Davis*.

Above: More than forty trains, both passenger and freight, once crossed today's Capitol Drive. Abundant signs and an art installation celebrate the history. *Burton Davis.*

Left: In 2010, a pedestrian bridge replaced the 1928 train trestle bridge over Capitol Drive. *Burton Davis.*

The trail starts to fill with exercisers early in the morning. *Burton Davis*.

The Milwaukee County Public Art Committee (MCPAC) commissioned this sculpture from artist Takashi Soga. *Burton Davis*.

Birth of the Oak Leaf

The Hank Aaron and Oak Leaf connected easily at three locations:

- Doyne Park west of the Miller Valley
- Discovery World at the lakefront
- Underwood Creek Parkway at 123rd Street and Bluemound Road in Wauwatosa

In addition, some maps appear to show a connection at South Eighty-Fourth Street, though it's difficult for a biker to access one trail from the other at this point. Here a rider has to use a series of local streets to go from one trail to the other.

In another part of the city, federal and state grants allowed land originally used to carry beer away from breweries to be converted to a recreation trail (aptly named the Beerline Trail). This provided a connection between the Riverwest neighborhood and downtown Milwaukee. Grants started providing money in 2002, and work progressed in sections. The four-thousand-foot trail officially opened in October 2010 with a ceremonial walk starting in Gordon Park.[104]

Most riders enjoying the trails clocked a few miles, but in September 2002, two friends made an ambitious trip around Lake Michigan via bicycle. The two had recently finished college and wanted to enjoy one last trip before facing the rest of adulthood. Matt Lawrenz described some of the preparation:

> *My friend and I had been doing a lot of biking around Milwaukee and different bike trails in Wisconsin for a few years. We would work up to doing fifty- to sixty-mile rides and had started a tradition of biking from Milwaukee to Madison along the Glacial Drumlin trail every summer, which is about one hundred miles I believe. We would make a three-day trip of it, taking one day to relax before returning on the third day. At some point during our riding around Milwaukee and parts of the Oak Leaf Trail, we noticed the signs for the Great Lakes Circle Tour or Lake Michigan Circle Tour. I think that sparked our imagination for making a grand trip around the lake. It was probably a couple years in the making and we prepared by doing a couple of short overnight trips fully loaded with gear, tent, etc. to practice and work out any bugs. Finally, in September of 2002, we accomplished the trip.*[105]

The circle tours were intended for automobiles, but the pair adapted the idea using various maps and the Harvey Botzman book *'Round Lake Michigan: A Bicyclist's Tour Guide*.[106] The pair started in Milwaukee and made a counterclockwise loop around the lake. Lawrenz rode a Cannondale mountain bike fitted with road tires and a rack with two panniers (storage bags sometimes called saddlebags).

> *Some of the best moments included biking in northern Michigan between Traverse City and the Straits of Mackinaw. There was some beautiful scenery during that stretch of the ride and a point where the road was high overlooking the lake and the weather was beautiful. We hadn't been to Michigan before and were unaware of some of the beautiful dunes and sandy beaches on that side of the lake, especially places like Ludington State Park. We had many adventures and surprises along the way, though. Since the trip, I've been back several times camping with my wife and now kids to enjoy more places, especially in the Traverse City area.*

In 2005, the Bicycle Federation of Wisconsin produced a biking map funded by the city and the county. Longtime biking advocate Dave Schlabowske, who had experience with previous maps, coordinated the project. At that time, the Oak Leaf Trail was 106 miles, with 48 miles of paved off-road paths, 31 miles of parkway drives and 27 miles on city streets. The map stated that portions on city streets "will eventually be converted to off-road paths."[107]

The Trails Council formed and began holding bimonthly meetings at the Milwaukee County Parks administration headquarters. Participants included parks employees and representatives of the National Park Service, DNR and City of Milwaukee; business owners; and citizen representatives who volunteered their time. Some members were nonvoting.

The council's mission was to advise the County Parks Department "toward a sustainable and enhanced regional trails network." Topics ranged far beyond the Oak Leaf Trail to encompass all county park trails, including activities like snowmobiling and kayakers using "water trails." The council advocated for a trails coordinator position with the county parks and also worked on snowplowing on the Oak Leaf.

Park funding was a huge concern for groups like members of the nonprofit Lake Park Friends. Joe Wilson, past president of the Friends, said in 2006, "We're basically just putting Band-Aids on a system that has been cut to the bone. We're losing a part of the social compact if we forget that these are the people's parks and they need to be maintained."[108] The county increasingly relied on private citizens to buttress a park system that had lost two-thirds of its workers and 64 percent of its inflation-adjusted tax levy between 1986 and 2006.

> ### EVEN A BIRD BIKED THE OAK LEAF TRAIL
>
> One of the creatures enjoying the Oak Leaf Trail is a yellow-naped Amazon parrot. His owner, Herb, built the bird a special cage and takes him out for stimulation. Herb said he takes Barney the Biking Bird to "the New Berlin Recreation Trail, the Oak Leaf, the Glacial Drumlin, he even gets to Door County and Peninsula State Park." Herb preferred that his last name be kept confidential, but he did share Barney's exploits at barneythebikingbird.com and handed out business cards with a Facebook page to the many people who stopped the pair to chat. By the fall of 2018, Herb and Barney had tabulated seventeen thousand miles, and the pair averaged about three thousand miles per year. Barney can only be outside when temperatures are between fifty and ninety degrees, while Herb can only bicycle when he does not have to work.

In 2008, the city held the first annual Pedestrian Safety Week. To help draw attention, it included volunteers dressed in giant sausage costumes, Bango from the Milwaukee Bucks basketball team and other mascots serving as high-visibility crossing guards. Volunteers passed out Streetshare brochures. The safety week was timed to coordinate with an International Walk to School date.[109]

In 2009, Milwaukee County Parks and Recreation won the national gold medal for excellence in parks management under park director Sue Black. Walkers and riders could visit beer gardens along the Oak Leaf such as the well-attended Estabrook Beer Garden, promoted as the first public beer garden in the United States since the Prohibition era. Beer garden visitors could happen upon a trail to hike in the future.

Near where Milwaukee attempted to hold its first marathon one December day in 1972, the city successfully hosted triathlons of national caliber. In August 2015, Team USA of USA Triathlon tweeted:

> *The city of Milwaukee has been an amazing host for Age Group Nationals over the past three years. The venue, set along the shores of Lake Michigan near the Milwaukee Art Museum and Discovery World, has been a favorite for many athletes—even winning Best Urban Triathlon through the Triathlon Business International Triathlete's Choice Awards in 2013.*[110]

Officials continued forward-looking planning and worked on the 2035 Park and Open Space Plan, which forecast millions of dollars in new park development over the next quarter-century and pointed out the maintenance backlog. The county park system included 15,000 acres and more than 150 parks.[111]

The Badgerland Striders helped people gauge the distance they went on the trail. Longtime Badgerland Striders member Marty Malin noticed markers at an out-of-state fun run and decided to mimic that on the Oak Leaf. After securing permission, he worked on flat granite markers that would not interfere with the county's grass mowing machines—drivers could send the machines right over the top of the markers.

> *My final idea, which I presented to the governing body of my running club, the Badgerland Striders, involved placing two colors of four-by-eight-inch granite blocks embedded in cement every half mile on both the main Oak Leaf Trail loop, and…on all of the spurs. We would install them so that every mile marker was one color, and the half mile markers were a different color. That way, a trail user would only have to glance at the color to see*

Runners enjoy the trail from dawn to dusk and throughout the seasons. *Eddee Daniel.*

Birth of the Oak Leaf

> *if they were on a full or half mile from where they started, so that if they turned around at that point, they would know if they were going to finish with an even or odd total mileage.*

Volunteers spent several years working to mark the whole trail and its spurs.

The county continued to add mileage to the trail, and in 2011, work began to link the Hank Aaron State Trail to Underwood Parkway. When completed, this allowed an experienced rider to go from Dane County's Cottage Grove to the Milwaukee lakefront using the Glacial Drumlin, New Berlin Recreational Trail, Hank Aaron and Oak Leaf. Riders could link the trails and be mostly off road for the significant distance.

The Park People of Milwaukee County introduced the Oak Leaf Discovery Tour at a 105 Days of Summer event in June 2012. This event celebrated Milwaukee County Parks' 105th anniversary.[112] Volunteers like Cheri Briscoe, chair of the Milwaukee County Parks Advisory Commission and volunteer with the nonprofit Park People, helped organize the fun challenge. Anyone could participate in the Oak Leaf Discovery Tour by obtaining a "passport" and using it to record keywords found throughout various parks. It developed into an annual event, and Wheel & Sprocket helped promote the passport at the company's bike expo through 2016. Winners were drawn at random from all submissions at a fall gathering. The Oak Leaf Discovery Tour continued through at least 2018.

Repairs on the aging asphalt from the late 1960s and 1970s continued. A section washed out from wave action in Bay View was resurfaced. In 2015, a large section of the well-traveled, well-loved South Shore Corridor in and near Grant Park and Sheridan Park was resurfaced, and some areas were rerouted. (A stretch in Warnimont Park was not included.) Local politicians such as Patricia Jursik advocated for funding. The Menomonee River Parkway got bridges and other improvements.

Trail users continued to include both individuals and small groups, including teams. John Danielson of Wauwatosa used the trail as the track and field assistant coach for distance for Divine Savior Holy Angels High School. His children attended the school, and he started coaching in 2011. He also used the trail for his own conditioning and ran on it nearly every day since about 1979, including in temperatures down to thirteen degrees below zero. He started running in college and kept up an impressive multiyear streak of daily running a mile or more, which he recorded on runeveryday.com. "I like to get out during the morning when I'm not coaching and I've got no worries in the world. I love the nature. On the trail I've seen coyotes,

Milwaukee County's Oak Leaf Trail

Trail users range from casual to more serious—but they all enjoy the view. *Author's collection.*

deer, rabbits, raccoons, foxes, snakes once in a while. In the summer, turtles, frogs," he said. Danielson encountered a deer that would watch him warm up. He lived in the village of Wauwatosa and frequented sections of the trail near Highway 100, Hart, Hoyt and Currie Parks and Menomonee Parkway or Little Menomonee Parkway. He appreciated when the county began arranging for plowing the off-road sections of the trail, since he regularly ran outside at least a mile.[113]

People continued to pound the trail for fun and to get the coveted runner's high. Couples met and friendships formed over shared interests in outdoor sports. "In high-use areas, the trail sees 1,200 people daily, and even in winter, 500 people a day still use it," said county parks trails coordinator Gage Brogan in 2017.[114] Patricia Jursik, Preserve Our Parks board member, Sheridan Park friends board member and former Milwaukee County supervisor, asserted in July 2018 that the trail was "the most used sport facility in Milwaukee County" and that it beat out big venues like Miller Park and the University of Wisconsin–Milwaukee Panther Arena. In a letter to the editor of the *Bay View Compass*, Jursik shared that while organized events make good use of the trail, "casual use by citizens accounts for most traffic—walkers, joggers, parents with perambulators, skate boarders, cross-country skiers, even children on trikes, and bird watchers." She went on to assert that the trail is neglected from a funding perspective.[115]

The Southeastern Wisconsin Regional Planning Commission participated in a 2015–2016 study to help gauge trail use with infrared counters. Federal Highway Administration money (plus a 20 percent local match) funded volume counts on the Oak Leaf and many other local trails via the Bicycle-Pedestrian Count Technology Pilot Project. Fourteen-day counts at five Oak Leaf Trail locations captured total trail volume, the average weekday use and average weekend use. The most popular point surveyed throughout Southeastern Wisconsin was on the Oak Leaf Trail east of the Menomonee River and west of Hart Park, a location with a total volume of 15,120, a weekday average of 960 and a weekend day average of 1,380. Automatic counters recorded these data from September 14, 2015, through September 27, 2015. This total volume nearly doubled the location with the second highest volume, which was the New Berlin Trail off 124th Street in Waukesha County.[116]

Experienced riders like Tom Held, a journalist on topics including biking and other silent sports, occasionally rode the whole perimeter of the Oak Leaf in a day. He shared in the *Journal Sentinel* online that "deteriorating pavement continues to be a problem on the Oak Leaf. In addition, sections of the trail that cover municipal streets and intersections could use a bit better signage, for wayfinding. Overall, however, I pedaled away from my circumnavigation largely impressed and plotting more day trips close to home."[117]

Organized rides and runs involving the Oak Leaf continued. These included various distances and sometimes corporate sponsors such as the Ride on the Wild Side, sponsored by Anthem Blue Cross & Blue Shield benefitting the Zoological Society of Milwaukee. A 2.5-mile kids' route stayed inside the zoo, but longer routes traversed portions of the Oak Leaf Trail.

After some ups and downs, the Interurban Trail opened in Ozaukee County and created a northern connection with the Oak Leaf. Some locals resisted the idea, but it eventually got completed.[118] A crucial aspect of the Interurban was a bike bridge over the interstate freeway. Business owner Chris Kegel, president of Wheel & Sprocket bike shop and Ozaukee County supervisor, was credited with helping make the bridge happen on the political front.[119] Kegel was a bike advocate locally with groups such as trail councils in Mequon and Milwaukee County and the Ozaukee Interurban Trail Advisory Council; on the state level with the Bicycle Federation of Wisconsin (where he served as a president and longtime board member), the Wisconsin Off Road Bicycling Association and the Wisconsin State Trails Council; and nationally with the International Mountain Bicycling Association, the Bikes Belong advocacy group (now named People for Bikes, where he was a founding member), the League of American Bicyclists, the National Bicycle Dealers Association and Recreation for Individuals Dedicated to the Environment.[120] The Wisconsin Bicycling Hall of Fame inducted him in 2017.

A ten-mile bike ride in honor of Chris Kegel sought to raise funds to improve wayfinding along the Oak Leaf. The concept was to color-code sections similar to the New York City Subway. The Chris Kegel Foundation worked with Milwaukee County Parks and the Bike Fed on this effort.[121] A new website at https://county.milwaukee.gov/EN/Parks/Explore/Trails/Oak-Leaf-Trail with color-coded sections called "branch lines" launched in September 2018, and a map was under development.

The popular section of the trail at the Root River Parkway got an extension that included a jaunt through the Rock Sports Complex, which already had a popular mountain biking trail. It ran along Old Loomis Road (parallel to Loomis Road), through the complex and across a bridge for bicyclists and pedestrians with a connection to the rest of the trail at Root River Parkway. "The majority of the project costs will be funded by an $860,000 Federal Transportation Alternatives Program grant, and the remaining 20 percent will be funded by matching county funds and an additional grant," wrote Tiffany Stoiber in the *Journal Sentinel*.[122]

Singer-songwriter John Stano, a resident of Milwaukee's Bay View neighborhood, created an original song that paid tribute to the trail. He called it "Meet Me on the Oak Leaf" and debuted it in the spring of 2018. He said, "When Jill told me about her book and asked me to write a companion song about the Oak Leaf Trail I was intrigued. I don't usually write to a prompt but I live just a few blocks from the trail and have logged many a mile there on foot, bike, and skis." Lyrics appear at the end of this book.

Using technology to help provide power became more popular—new designs called eBikes have a hub motor fitting on the front or rear wheel or a mid-drive motor at the middle of the bike. Riders purchased entirely new bikes that include power assist or bought aftermarket kits and added them to their current bikes. The eBikes were illegal to engage on the Oak Leaf Trail,

Birth of the Oak Leaf

A bridge opened in 2018 to connect the north side of the Rock Sports Complex to the Oak Leaf Trail. When the bridge opened, the path south of it remained under construction. *Gloria Rothenbueler.*

Children enjoy outings on the trail. *Jenna Stoll Photography.*

though bicycle advocates like Dave Schlabowske at the Bike Fed never heard of anyone getting a ticket for a violation.[123]

Elsewhere, some regulations did change to accommodate eBikes in certain situations. The Bike Fed worked with the DNR to allow eBikes traveling up to fifteen miles per hour on linear touring trails as codified in NR 45.05(3)(em).[124] This did not affect the Oak Leaf Trail and others outside DNR jurisdiction, where eBikes remained illegal unless operated only by human power. Attempts at broader regulations through state senate and assembly bills did not reach floor vote in 2018.[125]

By 2018, the trail was over 125 miles, combining dedicated paths, parkways shared with cars and standard roadways. Mature trees were plentiful along the route, a far cry from the late 1800s, when clearcutting left Milwaukee devoid of established trees. A website run by the county provided updates on closures and improvements and described the trail in segments called "lines" to help new riders orient themselves and explore new sections. The county park system entailed over 15,000 acres of parkland among 158 parks and 11 parkways. Rails-to-Trails Conservancy worked with seven southeastern counties of Wisconsin to develop the Route of the Badger, envisioned as a 500-mile system connecting 340 miles of existing trail.

New Bike Models and Helmets Reach Riders

Inventive people looking to get places faster and sell bicycles and components made inventions that contributed to safety, speed and efficiency.

The *hobby horse* bike had two same-sized wheels but lacked pedals or a drive chain. It was similar to today's youth "balance bikes," sometimes used by young children learning to ride.

Cycling was popular in France, and a Parisian manufactured the first steel-rimmed wheels with wire spokes. These were advantageous, because they were much lighter than wooden-spoked wheels. The move to steel allowed manufacturers to further increase the size of the driving wheel. The *velocipede* got closer to comfort riding but lacked pneumatic tires and a chain drive. As the authors point out in the bicycling history *The Dancing Chain: The History and Development of the Derailleur Bicycle*, "The first pedaled bicycles had front wheels 32-36 inches in diameter. Over the next few years, the size of front wheels would increase considerably to provide greater speed."[126] They dramatically increased to an astounding 60 inches on the front wheel of a high bicycle then came back down for safety and stability.

High wheels were uneven, with one huge wheel stabilized by a smaller wheel behind. They were difficult to mount and ride—and difficult to stop and dismount. On the other hand, they were picturesque, and many of their riders, mostly gentlemen with enough money to afford the expense of the bicycle and leisure time to ride it, dressed nicely in tweed clothing and turned heads as they rode. The very first riders made the newspaper just for riding down the street. People with long legs had a real advantage. Bicycle clubs naturally formed, precursors to clubs here still gathering for a snack and a ride on the Oak Leaf Trail. A few of these theatrical high wheel models are still rolling, and sometimes modern riders can be spotted in parades, still attracting attention.

Tricycles made an appearance and not just for children or elderly riders. They were more stable and dignified than their two-wheeled cousins but took up a lot of storage space. Early models had cranks on the front axle like today's versions ridden by toddlers. Later models improved with a crank moving a chain that turned real axles, making this easier to ride on rough roads. Embarking on a long journey by tricycle sounds silly to today's riders, but wealthy, dignified people did just that in the 1860s and 1870s.

Safety bicycles with pneumatic tires reached America in 1892, and models like the "Roger" had thirty-six-inch wheels and a central chain drive.[127] They would be familiar and rideable to today's adults. As the name indicates, these were easier to start, stop and maintain balance on, so they reached a much broader audience.

A *cruiser* bicycle (also known as beach cruiser or motorbike) has balloon tires, an upright seating posture, a single-speed drivetrain and sometimes extraneous style features like a faux gas tank. Cruisers were heavy and slow but easy to balance and ride. They were everywhere from the 1930s to 1950s. The wacky movie *Pee-Wee's Big Adventure* depicts Pee-Wee's quest to recapture a beloved stolen cruiser. Many people are nostalgic for them, like local Scott Wilke, who has collected them over the years and created an informal museum in the South Shore Cyclery bicycle shop in Cudahy. While the shop displays a variety of vintage bicycles, the focus is on American-made bicycles manufactured between 1933 and the late 1950s. Their warm spot in locals' hearts is evidenced in frequent requests to purchase models from the museum. As described earlier in this book, World War II spurred the government to designate twelve manufacturers who could produce slimmed-down Victory bicycles to certain specifications. By government order, all other bicycle manufacturing ceased.

In the 1970s, derailleur-equipped bikes offered ten speeds. The derailleur's impact on long rides over varied terrain is difficult to overstate, because it allowed riders to change gears while still pedaling, a huge advantage in hilly terrain. After decades of innovation for the elite riders, the derailleur reached the masses in "road bikes," known among casual riders as a ten-speed.

The next wave of bicycles included the sports roadster models or "English racer" for adults. These bikes were similar but had three gears instead of the cruiser's one gear. Kids got lowriders and muscle bikes.

Some adult riders considered road bikes too fussy and prone to flat tires. *Mountain bikes* were almost the opposite—rough and rugged. After smaller experiments by the military and civilians, modern mountain bikes were created to get riders down Mount Tamalpais in California and then mass marketed in the 1970s. These bike styles originated stateside versus mimicking European styles. Manufacturers had to react quickly to the major new style, which grew in sales until the peak in 1992. No single style replaced the mountain bike, with comfort bikes, commuter bikes, city bikes and even hybrids and tandems all competing for adult bikers' attention.

Helmets designed specifically for bicycling were not available until the 1970s. Before then, some cyclists tried pith helmets, and racing cyclists wore leather head covers or tight hats as a little protection against scrapes. Some riders eventually tried hockey helmets or motorcycle helmets, but they were heavy and never caught on. Some elite riders wore helmets for aerodynamics but not crash protection. In 1975, Bell Helmets Inc. started manufacturing a safety helmet specifically for bicycling. It had a polystyrene foam liner covered by a Lexan hard shell.[128] Parents encouraged children to wear helmets, and eventually adult helmets would be required in large races.

Electric bikes provide riders with an extra power boost thanks to a battery and motor. They enjoyed popularity in China and elsewhere before reaching the United States. They became popular locally around 2018, when sales jumped over the previous year.[129]

Part II

MILWAUKEE RIVER LINE

Brown Deer, Kletzsch, Lincoln, Estabrook, Lake, McKinley and Veterans Parks

Riders coming south along the Oak Leaf Trail's Milwaukee River Line enjoy a mix of converted rail lines and more natural paths that follow the geography. As riders or runners head downtown, they experience a mix of scenery and obstacles along the trail: near immersion in nature along meandering rivers, crossing some streets with heavy vehicular traffic such as Hampton Avenue, beautiful woods such as Cambridge Woods and historic parks with Lake Michigan views. Art mixes with nature, because the trail is dotted with large sculptures and historic statues.

The southern end is certainly the most "artsy" section of the trail, snaking trail users past several sculptures and then the dramatic Milwaukee Art Museum, an architectural landmark. This portion is popular with students, including those at the University of Wisconsin–Milwaukee; visitors to the Urban Ecology Center; commuters heading to jobs downtown in the heart of the business district; people sweating through training for an upcoming race; and those seeking a nature fix. Many never know the history they tread upon.

In 1966, local bicycling was about to go off road and off sidewalk. An idea to build designated paths for use by cyclists progressed through analysis and committees to the funding stage. The Committee on Parks and Recreation asked the Finance Committee to submit a recommendation to furnish $45,000 to match federal funds for a pilot program of two bicycle trails. (The other was built on the south side in Sheridan and Warnimont Parks in 1968 and is described in Part 3 of this book.) The county took an approach of one north-side and one south-side offering, a common twin approach to county offerings such as senior centers. The trails were funded in 1967, and these first paved paths helped gauge interest in the public use of bicycle trails.

Both sites were along the eastern edge of the county in historic parks. Since the county already owned the land on which it would build the trails, money was required only for surveying and construction. These two small-scale projects allowed the county to take advantage of federal funds to dip its toe into the new concept of bicycle paths.

The northern trail passed several landmarks still visible today. It began on the lakefront at the McKinley tennis courts, proceeded north on Lincoln Memorial Drive to Kenwood Avenue and then turned south to the crest of the bluff above the North Avenue Pumping Station. It was 3.1 miles, a useful distance for casual riders but hardly worth an outing for elite riders unless they repeated the loop to give themselves a true workout. It did not return a rider directly to the starting point. It was eight feet wide and blacktopped.

The county dedicated the new trail in October 1967 at McKinley Marina. A field director for the National Bicycle Institute from Chicago was on hand, arriving in town that Thursday and meeting with a reporter. He saw a strong future for local riding and even said, "Milwaukee may very well become the bicycle hub of the United States." He gave a plaque to Supervisor Joseph Greco for his work to get the trail created.[130] Greco rode a tandem or two-seat bike with another official at the dedication. He had sponsored an essay contest for children and gave the two winners each a bicycle.[131] About 350 people attended the opening dedication.

By October 19, the trail was being "heavily used" by a variety of people, according to a *Milwaukee Journal* article. It described everyone from "tykes on tricycles to grandfatherly types" using the trail. The trail description shared newspaper pages filled with University of Wisconsin student antiwar protests, debates over open housing ordinances and Milwaukee's failure to attract a new major-league baseball team.[132] Perhaps a getaway to nature helped some riders take their minds off these issues.

The paths were designed and posted with signs exclusive to biking—not roller skating or other activities. Not until many decades later would the trails be officially considered multiuse—for walking, jogging, skateboarding, rollerblading and other activities. Through intergovernmental cooperation, patience and advocacy, a few miles would grow into a well-known bike trail of over 125 miles. This small portion would become a key piece in that trail's section, named the Milwaukee River Line for its watery eponym. The Milwaukee River Line's northernmost park is Brown Deer.

BROWN DEER PARK

At the north end of the line is Brown Deer Park. Brown Deer has its share of bicyclists today but was once a veritable hotspot for a different style of cycling, track racing. Brown Deer Park had a banked track, or velodrome, for decades, and it was even the site of two Olympic qualifying races. Brown Deer's velodrome was a four-hundred-meter track with minimal banking that required riders to learn a specific cornering skill or risk flying off the track and even into the parking lot.[133]

Over the decades, the velodrome deteriorated, and by the 1960s, the Milwaukee County Board of Supervisors was plotting how to keep the sport alive in the area. It considered a swimming pool at the site of Brown Deer's velodrome and a new velodrome in Wilson Park off Howard Avenue on Milwaukee's south side. (Wilson never got a velodrome and is now known for its pool, senior center and ice arena seating two thousand.)

In 1975, velodromes were getting scarce across the country.[134] Only a dozen paved tracks existed, and two were in Wisconsin—Brown Deer and Kenosha. Brown Deer's was condemned by 1980, as the County Board of Supervisors described: "The Brown Deer Park racing track is the second oldest of its kind in the United States and has been condemned because it is too shallow (and thus unsafe) for more than one rider at a time." The county board required "the Director of Parks, Recreation and Culture to evaluate the existing track and also study the feasibility of developing a national competitive caliber bicycle racing track to be located in Brown Deer Park at the site of the existing track."[135] It never transpired but didn't completely die off.

The Milwaukee County velodrome idea resurfaced in the 1990s in the Mayor's Bicycle Task Force, but Brown Deer never got another velodrome, requiring track cyclists to drive long distances to reach another venue. Most of them headed to Kenosha, which has the country's oldest operating velodrome. It was a long drive after work and made track riding less feasible for Milwaukee County residents. During the Brown Deer velodrome days, interest in track racing certainly had a contagion effect that kept locals interested in bicycling. These riders would encourage friends and family to pick up the hobby.

Bicycle trails surely weren't a slam dunk in Brown Deer. In 1979, the park commission studied a recreation trail along Wisconsin Electric Power Company right-of-way in Brown Deer. It had been requested by Supervisor Robert L. Jackson Jr. The commission decided that "the proposed portion

> ## Track Riders Head Down to Kenosha
>
> The Washington Park Velodrome opened in July 1927 and is owned by the Kenosha Parks Department, while a nonprofit organization governs it. Cyclists rode on asphalt until 2015, when Kenosha spent $700,000 on upgrades that included changing to a concrete surface. Cracks in the concrete required rework in 2016. The venue is nicknamed the "Bowl" and has hosted several national championships.[136] As of 2018, it was one of about two dozen left in the country.

of the bike trail not be implemented at this time."[137] County Board of Supervisors proceedings do not indicate a reason.

Today, Brown Deer contains a popular section of trail that branches off the Milwaukee River Line and provides a direct, off-road connection to Estabrook Park following a converted railroad right-of-way. This part of the Oak Leaf is named for bicycling advocate Harold "Zip" Morgan, who first laid and helped popularize a sixty-four-mile trail in 1939 as described in earlier in this book.

Traveling south, the trail heads toward Kletzsch Park.

KLETZSCH PARK

Prior to European settlers reaching the area, Native Americans from several different tribes traversed what is now Kletzsch Park. Increase Lapham, sometimes referred to as the state's first great scientist, documented that successive groups of native people buried their dead near the river.[138] He documented evidence of cultivation he called "ancient garden-beds" and "Indian corn-hills." The park still has an exceptional grouping of native plants and is known for good salmon fishing.

The park is named for hotel owner and real estate investor Alvin P. Kletzsch, who was among other notable names as the first set of volunteer park commissioners. He served a long tenure—1907 through 1941. This well-rounded individual became the University of Wisconsin's first football coach in 1887.[139]

> *The history of the land as a public park began in 1918, when the 35 acre Blatz farm was purchased. The Pierron farm, a 45 acre parcel to the north of the Blatz land, was acquired in 1927. Since these parcels were not contiguous, two separate parks existed. The fissure was healed when the 15 acres between the sites was acquired in 1929, creating the 118.9 acre park we know today.*[140]

In the 1930s, swimmers flocked to Kletzsch Park and enjoyed a pond made by contractors plus a beach and a bathhouse. As described in the Estabrook section of this book, the park benefitted from work by the Civilian Conservation Corps (CCC) relief programs. CCC crews also built the impressive park shelter. Decades later, in the mid-1970s, the area would get its portion of the bicycle trail.

LINCOLN PARK

Lincoln Park is a major asset in the extensive Milwaukee County park system. It's over three hundred wooded acres with a picturesque river, golf course and aquatic center. The David F. Schulz Aquatic Center contains the only deep well pool open in 2018 on the city's north side and also has an attraction called a "lazy river" on which people enjoy floating. It is named for a Milwaukee native who worked as a bureaucrat in Chicago, then returned to Milwaukee as budget director for the county, served a short stint as parks director and served a one-year term as county supervisor.[141] The area has a long history as another popular swimming spot—the City of Milwaukee provided swimming facilities during the early 1920s when the river, not Lake Michigan, was the go-to spot for a cool dip. Eventually, pollution in the river led to heavier use of pools and the lake.[142]

The county took another big step in expanding riding in the Milwaukee River Corridor with several sections in 1975:

> *WHEREAS Milwaukee County is interested in developing outdoor recreational facilities on the following described projects for the enjoyment of the citizenry of said Milwaukee County and the State of Wisconsin: The development of a bicycle trail along the Lincoln Creek from Lincoln Park to North 60th Street and the West Hampton Avenue; the development of a bicycle trail along the Little Menomonee River Parkway from West*

The trail swings alongside picturesque views of the Milwaukee River in Lincoln Park. *Author's collection.*

Hampton Avenue to West Good Hope Road; and the development of an extension to the Milwaukee River Bicycle Trail along the old Chicago and Northwestern Railroad right-of-way from the flushing tunnel at the Lakefront to Estabrook Park.[143]

The supervisors budgeted a total of $275,000 ($87,000 for Lincoln Creek, $93,500 for Little Menomonee Trail and $95,000 for Milwaukee River Trail) and authorized applications to the DNR for these projects. Today's runners and riders on the Oak Leaf Trail in Lincoln Park can choose a straight-as-a-surveyor's-line route along a converted rail line that connects to

Brown Deer Park or take a more meandering path along a beautiful stretch of the Milwaukee River. The river portion goes right past a large, bright-red sculpture. It's about fourteen feet by twenty-four feet by six feet and sits on the east side of the path near the aquatic center—its size and bright color make it hard to miss. The Milwaukee County Public Art Committee (MCPAC) commissioned it, and artist Takashi Soga installed it in May 2010.[144] The effort was part of Milwaukee County's Percent-for-Art program, in which art projects are commissioned in conjunction with major projects.

Those near the river navigate past a golf course at 1000 West Hampton Avenue. The course opened with six holes in 1912 and was subsequently modified several times. It became a bona fide nine holes in 1922. In the 1960s, it had to fit around the huge freeway being constructed and got a makeover.[145] Trail users heading clockwise cross under Interstate 43 and then the busy Hampton Avenue to reach Estabrook Park.

LINCOLN CREEK PARKWAY CLOSING TIME

A security scare in the late 1970s caused concern about the Lincoln Creek Parkway:

> *WHEREAS, a number of muggings, thefts and other criminal acts frowned upon by our community and in violation of our county ordinances have been occurring at an epidemic rate in our county park system; and*
> *WHEREAS, the latest such behavior erupted in the Lincoln Creek Parkway necessitating county and city officials to hold a meeting with the County Sheriff, City Police representatives and residents of the area in an attempt to put an end to the violations.*[146]

Supervisors unanimously approved an adjustment in the Lincoln Creek Parkway's closing time from midnight to 10:00 p.m. It affected pedestrian and bicycle traffic, and the supervisors planned for signs to be posted. No further flare-ups that year were recorded in the County Board of Supervisors proceedings, though they do mention rowdy activity in the Root River Parkway.

ESTABROOK PARK

This park is named after Charles E. Estabrook, first secretary of the Milwaukee County Park Commission, who served from 1907 until 1918. Like many Milwaukee parks, the land was once the site of heavy industry. Here industry included a cement company, which took advantage of the rock to create a needed building supply. The purchase of eighty-three acres from the cement company, the largest parcel in a series of acquisitions, formed the cornerstone of today's Estabrook Park.

In the mid-1920s, the park contained a tourist camp and a ballfield. People could access the park via an unpaved roadway. The county landscape architect prepared a general development plan, and workers from various relief programs developed the park in the early and mid-1930s. They addressed flooding, which had flared up in 1924, built a control dam and removed approximately one hundred thousand cubic yards of limestone from the river.[147]

Relief labor programs in 1931 also developed beaches and bathhouses at Estabrook and Kletzsch Parks, taking advantage of the Milwaukee River. Its temperature was more bearable than the chilly Lake Michigan. They were very well used by the citizens, especially Kletzsch Park, which had the advantage of lights. As many as to 1,500 to 3,000 swimmers used Kletzsch Park to escape the heat on hot nights. People cooled off at swimming areas at Estabrook, Kletzsch and Gordon Parks along the Milwaukee River, plus private swimming areas.[148]

Due to pollution and deterioration of the bathhouse, 1945 was the last year the swimming area operated.[149] At Estabrook today, modern walkways encourage people to explore near the water. Riders and runners using the trail can often spot a few people fishing but no swimmers.

Today, trail users in Estabrook can choose to either hug the river on the western portion of the Oak Leaf Trail or enjoy an eastern fork. If they stay to the west on a summer evening, they experience a bipolar mix of beautiful nature and a hopping beer garden right alongside the trail. This was the first public beer garden since Prohibition and was eventually followed by beer gardens in other parks along the trail such as Humboldt, South Shore and Whitnall. The trail also goes near a dog park, sporting fields and a disc golf course.

Within Estabrook Park, a dramatic white building with four columns along the Oak Leaf Trail just north of Capitol Drive looks like it could be an old train station. In fact, it was a private home that Works Progress

Milwaukee River Line

The Milwaukee River, a few steps west of the Oak Leaf Trail in Estabrook Park, offers inspiring views. It's one of many places where the trail brings people alongside beautiful rivers. *Author's collection.*

Administration workers restored and relocated to the park in 1938. Benjamin Church, a carpenter, originally built the home in Kilbourntown, one of the three settlements that merged to form Milwaukee. It has been on the National Register of Historic Places since 1972 and is occasionally open to the public.

Some of the trail within Estabrook Park is converted railroad right-of-way. At the north side of Capitol Drive, east of the Oak Leaf Trail, the curious rider or runner can find a small abandoned section of railroad track among the flora and fauna. Squirrels scamper across track that once carried high-speed trains, and trees grow through the rails, allowing nature to overtake this castaway. The section between Juneau and Estabrook Parks was once gravel.[150]

This area was once populated by Native Americans, of course, and then became an apple orchard owned by Thomas Bare (or Baer). The railroad got an easement to lay track through his property, and he wasn't happy that work began before he got paid for the easement. He drove railroad

The trail passes a beer garden. It can be a fun rest stop and occasionally a source of polka music. *Burton Davis.*

workers off his land at gunpoint. Eventually, he was paid, and the track was completed.[151]

The first train came through the area in 1873, and it roughly followed the Milwaukee River. For the next hundred years, train whistles mixed into the everyday sounds of local life. The Chicago & Northwestern company called it the Airline Division, which connected Milwaukee to Fond du Lac, Wisconsin, west of the Kettle Moraine on the south end of Lake Winnebago. The track's right-of-way inadvertently provided an excellent route for the future trail.

The track eventually carried more than forty trains, both passenger and freight, every day. Popular freight included cement from the Milwaukee Cement Company, which operated on the banks of the river, and ice harvested from it. Downstream breweries used the ice in beer production. The railroad crossed a street, so automobile drivers had to wait every time they crossed paths with a train. In 1927, the Chicago & Northwestern authorized an underpass and trestle at today's Capitol Drive, then Atwater Road.[152] The sturdy bridge remained for decades.

One of the fastest passenger trains crossed that trestle bridge from 1935 to 1963. Bicycle riders may think they are cruising fast, but they are no match for the speed of the bright yellow and green train that made two passes per day across the track in this area. The train covered about four hundred miles between Minneapolis and Chicago in about four hundred minutes, so it was called the Twin Cities 400. It stopped in Shorewood until 1932. From that year until 1963, it continued to pass through the area without stopping.

The Capitol Drive section of the trail got interesting in 2010, when a designer created one of the most unique pieces of public art along the trail: the Ghost Train. This installation mimics the lighting and sound a bystander would experience when the Twin Cities 400 sped past. Marty Peck of Creative Lighting Design & Engineering designed the Ghost Train, and the Shorewood Public Art Committee coordinated the project. A long list of private donors helped finance it. The Ghost Train schedule changes with the seasons and is listed in the nearby bicycle-friendly Corner Bakery restaurant or at the website villageofshorewood.org. Signs along the Oak Leaf Trail explain the art installation and history of the railroad. The work was completed in conjunction with the reconstruction of Capitol Drive.

South of this section, runners and riders enjoy a very straight portion of the trail. Its lack of contour is a telltale sign that it is converted railroad right-of-way. In 1922, Shorewood's village president, William J. Hubbard, purchased this land.[153] Between the west side of the trail and the river are the Community Lodge (now called the Shorewood River Club) and the picturesque Hubbard Park Lodge. The latter was designed for Boy Scouts and Girl Scouts and was aptly nicknamed the "Scoutcraft Cabin." One can easily imagine outdoorsy folks enjoying it in days gone by with its cathedral ceiling, stone fireplace and balcony. Its rustic feel is just right for the popular local tradition of Friday fish fries. It also hosts weddings, Sunday brunch and other events. It's located one and a half blocks south of Capitol Drive and one block west of Oakland Avenue at 3565 North Morris Boulevard.

An automatic trail counter in this area captured traffic levels from July 28, 2014, through March 4, 2015. Peak days were Saturday, August 9, 2014

Large Railroad Facility

In the Menomonee Valley to the west of downtown, the Milwaukee Road center was the third-largest railroad facility in the world at 160 acres. There, workers built and repaired train cars. In fact, those workers constructed the Hiawatha streamliners that connected Chicago and the Twin Cities.[154]

(3,121 counted); Saturday, August 23, 2014 (3,113 counted); and Sunday, November 2, 2014 (2,991 counted). Even in the cold month of February, an average of 133 users were counted. In July, an average of 1,777 were counted each day.[155]

Sports have been popular in this area for a long time. The river once hosted huge events organized by canoe clubs. In 1938, a Venetian night water carnival drew fifty thousand people to watch events on the water, and a contest drew fifteen thousand:

> *Contests between canoe clubs were popular events. In 1938, for example, more than 15,000 attended the two-day* Milwaukee Journal *water sports show, held on the river between Kern and Hubbard parks. In addition to rowing races, that event included half- and one-mile marathon swimming contests and was capped by a motor boat race.*[156]

The five acres now occupied by Hubbard Park are part of a larger parcel the U.S. government bought from the Menomonee tribe in 1832.[157] The land once housed a variety of businesses, including a resort that had a succession of names: Lueddemann's-on-the-River in 1872, Zweitusch's Mineral Springs in 1873, Coney Island Park, Wonderland Amusement Park in 1905 and Ravenna in 1909. The last owners added a motorcycle track called the Milwaukee Motordrome. Today, the area's serenity belies its fun-filled past.

> *By any standard, the park was extremely successful. Patrons from all over the country would arrive by streetcar, which dropped them off at the Oakland Avenue and Menlo Boulevard gate. Visitors would be greeted by a whole host of rides, including a giant water slide and a tower off which dare-devils could jump and land on a trampoline below. The attraction drew in thousands of visitors every year. In fact, the popularity of the attraction would lead to the area declaring its independence from the Town of Milwaukee.*[158]

The area also once housed a thriving ice harvesting business. Ice was essential to one of the biggest industries in town: breweries. It also kept slaughterhouse storage areas cool. The Joseph Schlitz brewery ran ice harvesting in today's Cambridge Woods. The brewery owned parcels on both sides of the river and donated an eight-acre parcel on the river's east side that became parkland. Curious bikers and runners can still find evidence of the industries: remnants of a timber dam still sit on the river between North

Avenue and Capitol Drive, and tunnels built as underpasses by the railroad company still cross the Oak Leaf. Trail users are traversing right on top of the most notable remnant of historic industries: the railroad right-of-way.

The Village of Shorewood demonstrated its commitment to bicycling and walking with the Pedestrian & Bicycle Safety Committee, comprising seven citizens and a village liaison.[159] The group created a master plan in 2015.

Farther south near Gordon Park, the newer Beerline Trail runs along the west side of the river, while the older tail is on the east side. Gordon Park and its eastern neighbor, Riverside, hosted a lot of fun during the early 1900s.

Riders continuing south pass west of the University of Wisconsin–Milwaukee and through Cambridge Woods, a thin strip of twenty acres along the east side of the river. Then they reach the Urban Ecology Center's Riverside Park location. It's one of three locations for this nonprofit dedicated to environmental education that seeks to get people of all ages out into nature. The center has interesting architectural features along the trail and a pedestrian bridge across it. Employees make good use of the trail and incorporate it in their programming. Jamie Ferschinger, branch manager, told a writer for *Rails-to-Trails* magazine, "It's a green corridor from the river in the park down to the lake, so it's a great place to talk about river ecology and lake ecology, as well as native species and invasive species. Everything from small insects to big concepts can be taught along the Oak Leaf Trail."[160]

Locals developed traditions centering around the Oak Leaf. Some families enjoyed the trail together on the weekend. Shorewood residents Paul and Doris Dix have commuted to work downtown and also rode portions of the trail for fun with their two children. Doris has fond memories of combining a family ride on the Oak Leaf Trail with a sugary treat. As she described:

> *We have two daughters and they are three years apart, so, to convince the younger daughter to bike we used to go to Sil's near North Avenue. We'd bike down there and share a bag of mini donuts. This was when the girls were about six or seven and nine or ten. We'd go there, order the donuts, watch them be made, and get something to drink. We would sit on the little benches to eat them.*
>
> *Everyone is so friendly on the trail—the runners, the bikers, the old people walking in the morning. Everyone looks like they are enjoying the time outside.*

Jeff Wagner was using the trail in a very different way—he commuted in all seasons and went six and a half miles each direction. He used to alternate biking and running but later switched to consistently riding. He shared that "I once rode my Razor scooter which was way harder than I anticipated." On morning commutes, he routinely passed the same person doing yoga in the same spot near North Avenue and occasional people who had slept in the park. Among his favorite aspects were "being able to ride car free for miles" and "riding on fresh snow before it gets packed and icy." On weekends, he and his wife would bike south to Veterans Park for a picnic. When they had children, they repeated the tradition.[161]

Riders continuing clockwise reach Back Bay Park and, to its north, the historic Lake Park.

LAKE PARK

Lake Park, north of downtown but not quite to the village of Shorewood, has noble roots. It was designed by famous architect Frederick Law Olmsted, features a picturesque lighthouse along a great view of Lake Michigan, is populated by gorgeous trees and is surrounded by large, beautiful homes. By 1892, Lake Park was pieced together by acquisitions from various property owners (Jane Wright, G.A. Lueddemann, W. Weightman, the Gilman estate, Edward Barber and Lakeside Land Company) at a total cost of $255,175 for about 124 acres. At the northern end of today's Lake Park, the Lueddemann family operated a popular summer resort with scenic groves called Lueddemann's-on-the-Lake.

In 1835, the first U.S. government survey found the land of what is now Lake Park to be "well timbered" with native oaks, sugar maple, basswood, beech, hickory, elm, white ash, aspen and ironwood.[162] People enjoying the park today would probably describe it as full of trees. But extensive cutting, common throughout the Milwaukee area, once left the area barren. Luckily, civic-minded individuals worked to replenish and nourish the trees.

A lighthouse was built in 1855 on the edge of the bluff to signal ships on the lake. By 1879, erosion of the bluff made it necessary to move the tower one hundred feet inland. Trees were planted and nurtured, eventually growing so vigorously that the beam from the North Point lighthouse, on park property, was obscured by the leaves. The trees enjoyed by so many of today's trail users had become a safety hazard. In 1912, workers installed a new thirty-six-foot base of riveted steel for the lighthouse tower, and its beam was again visible to ships on Lake Michigan.

The lighthouse, built in 1879, was moved one hundred feet inland and then eventually raised onto a new base. It's a picturesque aspect of Lake Park. *Pixabay, Charlie Yoon.*

Today, the Oak Leaf Trail's runners and walkers enjoy a park full of trees, including the oak the bicycling and running path would eventually be named after. Oak is probably the most plentiful genus in the park. And it's certainly not true that if you've seen one oak, you've seen them all.

> *There are probably more large Oaks than any other genus of trees in the park. They fall into two categories: White and Red Oak types. The former has leaves with rounded lobes and relatively tasty acorns, while the Red Oaks have pointed bristle-tipped lobes and lousy tasting acorns. The two species of White Oaks are White Oak (*Quercus alba*), which constitute some of the largest and oldest trees in the park, and Swamp White Oak (*Quercus bicolor*), a wetland tree. There are many native Northern Red Oak (*Quercus rubra*) in the natural areas. Some small Pin Oak (*Quercus palustris*) have been planted.*[163]

The local park system has long benefitted from dedicated volunteers. Christian Wahl made significant contributions to the park when he retired from a glue factory he and his brother operated in Chicago then

> ### Don't Fence Me In
>
> Most people enjoy the trees, but some see them as nuisances. In 2001, a Wahl Avenue resident was annoyed that trees in Lake Park were obscuring his view of Lake Michigan. Thomas "the Lumberjack" Ewart cut down eighteen trees and faced criminal charges. In his defense, deed restrictions for residents provided an unrestricted view of the lake. He was fined $2,500 and paid legal fees of $55,000.

began a second career as a full-time volunteer. He lived near Lake Park on Prospect Avenue. Eventually, Wahl Avenue was named after him to honor his service as president of the board of park commissioners. (As Carl Baehr tells it, the honor helped gracefully usher him out of his role. He seems to have been disliked as a micromanager.[164]) The street now bearing his name is graced with beautiful homes. It was formerly called Park Place. Thanks to his volunteerism, he is sometimes identified as the father of Milwaukee's park system or its grandfather.[165] Today, friends groups carry on this thrust and voluntarily help steward the overall park and the trail system.

Today's trail users have free, unfettered access to a park that was once guarded by toll. No tollgates were permitted within the city of Milwaukee after the acceptance of the city charter in 1846, but a tollgate at the intersection of Park Place and Lake Avenue charged entrance fees into the park. Park commissioners wrote a letter to the president of the tollgate company, who removed one of two gates. Bicycles paid the lowest round-trip toll at five cents. Automobiles paid twenty cents for a round-trip. The nuisance ended when the park commission bought the lane on which the second gate was located.[166]

In 1929, Lincoln Memorial drive was constructed and passed the park at its north end, where the drive connected with East Kenwood Boulevard. Eventually, Oak Leaf Trail riders could choose a more westerly route through the park or a more easterly pair of trails near the lakefront. In the 1970s and 1980s, two roads within Lake Park, West Drive and Inner Park Drive, were closed to vehicles. They remain closed today, used by only bicyclists and pedestrians.[167]

Farther south, the Chicago & Northwestern Lake Front Depot once anchored the east end of Wisconsin Avenue. This impressive redbrick train station had a 234-foot clock tower and functioned as a gateway to the city.

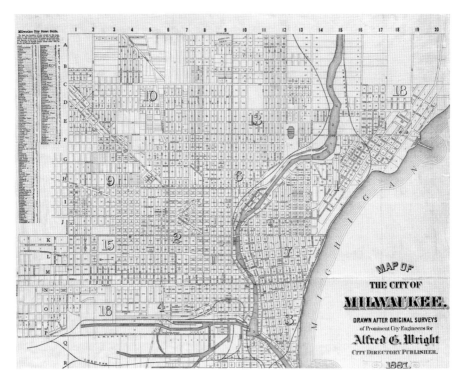

This 1887 city map shows rail lines, which eventually became recreation trails. Landfill extended the eastern edge of the shoreline and created parkland still heavily used today. *Lionel Pincus and Princess Firyal Map Division, New York Public Library.*

In 1964, Milwaukee County purchased it and surrounding land for the Lake Freeway.[168] Though this freeway did not transpire as planned, the depot was demolished in 1968.[169] As the railroad's influence on this part of Milwaukee's lakefront crumbled, bicycling enjoyed an upswing. Both types of transportation rely on long stretches of land to be successful. The writer of a park commission 1972 feasibility study pointed out that a trail of crushed gravel used a railroad right-of-way:

> *The Chicago and Northwestern Railroad right-of-way provides a lineal environment for cycling. The Park Commission is making the first use of this property which is eventually earmarked for rapid transit. The right-of-way crosses the upper East side of Milwaukee and terminates at the Lakefront. The gives the cyclist an option from the heavily traveled arteries of the City. Access points are provided near the University of Wisconsin–Milwaukee as well as several other points along the way. The Chicago and*

Milwaukee County's Oak Leaf Trail

Northwestern Railroad still operates a weekly rail service to some customers along the track, therefore, safety fencing was provided between the operating track and the bike trail. The trail is eight feet in width as all county trails are, however, it is surfaced with bound crushed stone instead of asphalt.[170]

Eventually, this would be paved and become a cherished section of the Milwaukee River Line.

North of the former Lake Front Depot and east of Lincoln Memorial Drive is Veterans Park. The large park includes yacht clubs, a memorial with a statue of General Douglas MacArthur, the Southeastern Wisconsin Vietnam Veterans Memorial and a lagoon. The Gift of Wings offers kites for sale, snacks and a variety of bike rentals. Walks for nonprofit groups often conclude in the park, and events such as parties commemorating Harley-Davidson motorcycle company's anniversary are often held there. Large crowds occupy the park for Independence Day fireworks.

War Memorial Center and Art Museum

Finnish American architect Eero Saarinen designed the Milwaukee County War Memorial Center. Its creation is another story of interorganizational collaboration, because the Milwaukee Civic Alliance joined fund-raising forces with three women's clubs: the Altrusa Club, the Business and Professional Women's Club and the Zonta Club of Milwaukee. The building at 740 North Lincoln Memorial Drive houses a group dedicated to a mission to "Honor the Dead. Serve the Living."

The center is part of the Milwaukee Art Museum, with nearly twenty-five thousand works of art and almost four hundred thousand yearly visitors. Its buildings include the war memorial, Quadracci Pavilion and Cudahy Gardens. Trail users cannot miss the Spanish architect Santiago Calatrava's dramatic white design, which opened in 2001. Most stop for a picture or two near the building. Large pieces spanning 217 feet look like the building's "wings" but are officially called the Burke Brise Soleil. It unfolds and collapses twice daily to act as a sunscreen. A pedestrian suspension bridge called the Reiman Bridge connects the museum to nearby sidewalks along office towers. Landscape architect Dan Kiley's design of fountains, grassy gardens and plazas complement the building.

The area's first bicycle messenger got a start near this area at just twelve years old. He proved himself faster than people on foot and those riding horses, and Western Union Telegraph Company hired him as a messenger. The Western Union office is long gone, but the address is 219 East Michigan Street.[171] The child, Edward Steichen, grew up to become a renowned photographer.

1972 U.S. ROAD RACING CHAMPIONSHIPS

Elite bicyclists from around the country rode this area on many occasions, and one was the 1972 U.S. Road Racing Championships, which also functioned as Olympic qualifiers. Races like these helped show enthusiasm for bicycling (even though the participants were Olympic-caliber or similar upper-echelon athletes, while most bicyclists were amateurs). City of Milwaukee resident Otto Wenz, eventual president of the U.S. Cycling Federation, helped organize the 1972 championships, subsequent championships held in Milwaukee and many other elite races in the area and nation. He began the Super Week series, which operated in the 1970s and 1980s and evolved into the Tour of America's Dairyland. On the national level, he helped draw the Junior World Championships to Allentown, Pennsylvania, after the race had been abroad for over sixty years and chaired the 1986 World Cycling Championships in Colorado Springs, Colorado.[172] He died in 2016, one year before being inducted into the Wisconsin Bicycling Hall of Fame.

The county board members welcomed the 1972 championship event and the modest tourism it would draw. The local chapter of the bicycling club called the Wheelmen helped organize. (Early bicycles were called "wheels," and their riders were called "wheelmen." They first formed a club in 1880.)

> *WHEREAS, the Milwaukee Wheelmen have received a commitment to hold the United States Road Racing Championships in Milwaukee on August 5 and August 6, 1972; and*
> *WHEREAS, said meet will attract 500–600 persons, including 175–200 competitors to our community, which meet will be the deciding factor on who will represent the United States in the Olympic Games; and*
> *WHEREAS, Otto Wenz, of 2607 N Downer Avenue, in Milwaukee, Chairman of the meet event, has requested that Milwaukee County facilities*

be utilized to conduct the meet over a four mile course on Milwaukee's East Side; now, therefore,
BE IT RESOLVED, That the staff of Milwaukee County Government and the County Park Commission be authorized and directed to cooperate with the Milwaukee Wheelmen in their handling of America's finest bicycle racing meet on August 5th and 6th, 1972 in Lake Park, the surrounding surface streets of North Lake Drive, North Terrace Avenue, North Wahl Avenue, the McKinley Park Hill, and North Lincoln Memorial Drive; and
BE IT FURTHER RESOLVED, That Milwaukee County extends an official welcome to all participants in the United States Road Racing Championships.[173]

The winners from Milwaukee's competition went to the infamous summer Olympics in Munich, West Germany, from August 26 to September 11, 1972. That year's cycling team included a local suburbanite, Jim Ochowicz of New Berlin.[174] Organizers aimed to host *Die Heiteren Spiele* or "the cheerful games," but the peaceful spirit of international competition was shattered by Palestinian terrorists. They killed eleven Israeli Olympians plus a West German police officer. Fifteen male athletes from the United States raced in road and track cycling events but did not medal. No women from any country competed.

Olympic-caliber riders helped inspire everyday folks to take up the sport. By the 1970s, thousands of bicyclists per year enjoyed the short experimental route in Lake Park. In the autumn of 1972, organizers made the sensible move of creating a loop by incorporating the steep Ravine Road.[175] Only some signage and curb changes were needed. (Bicyclists would sweat their way up the hilly road for decades until both the road and the bridge above it closed due to needed structural improvement.[176]) Signs were added to help make an enclosed loop clear to riders, and this included Terrace Avenue from North Avenue to Lafayette Street and Lafayette Avenue from Terrace Avenue west to Lake Drive and down the bluff to the McKinley tennis courts.[177]

In 1972, the trail system in the parks was getting national attention, and politicians were ready to further improve it. Supervisors directed the park commission to conduct a feasibility study for constructing a bike path. It would proceed from the Milwaukee County War Memorial Center, which had opened in 1957, northward along the Northwestern Railroad right-of-way through several parks—Riverside, Hubbard, Estabrook and Lincoln Park and Parkway—to North Sixtieth Street and West Hampton Avenue.

On May 25, 1972, the county board granted permission to negotiate for this land.[178] When completed, it would give commuters from Milwaukee's East Side, Shorewood, Whitefish Bay and beyond an uninterrupted commute to downtown employers.

In 1975, the county improved the signs and access ramps to sidewalks on the Lake Park bicycle trail. Access ramps allowed riders to ride up a ramp rather than maneuver across a curb. Signs designated the trail on North Terrace Avenue from East North Avenue to East Lafayette Place and on East Lafayette Place from North Terrace Avenue west to North Lake Drive. The city and county cooperated on these small improvements.[179]

The lakefront portions of the trail were always very popular. In 1976, the county hadn't figured out a reliable way to count users, and a parks landscape architect said automatic counters were often stolen. However, he said the two lakefront sections were most popular: Lake and Juneau Parks plus the eventual South Shore Corridor in South Shore, Bay View, Sheridan, Grant and Warnimont Parks.[180]

The area's trail got a boost in 1991, when the parks department applied for five projects and received funding for two. One of these would help further expand the bike trail. As reported in County Board of Supervisors proceedings:

> *WHEREAS, the Parks Department submitted five applications of which two, the Government Pier Walkway Development project and the Lakeside Bike Trail Development project competed successfully; now, therefore,*
> *BE IT RESOLVED, that the Director of Parks, Recreation and Culture is hereby authorized to enter into an Agreement with the State of Wisconsin Department of Natural Resources to accept a grant of $25,000 ($12,500 County/$12,500 State) for the Government Pier project and a grant of $80,000 ($40,000 County/$40,000 State) for the Lakeside Bike Trail project.*[181]

ENCROACHMENT CONCERNS

Occasionally, a private landowner would encroach on park land, including the trail. The Lowenberg-Fitch Partnership developed the Landmark on the Lake complex at the east end of Brady Street at 1660 North Prospect Avenue, on the valuable lakefront bluff in view of downtown skyscrapers, the marina, the art museum and surrounding park land. It placed fill on a portion of park land adjacent to the 76 Trail without obtaining permission. The County Board of Supervisors voiced concerns about the results: "If the Landmark project proceeds as originally proposed, County property will continue to be plagued with erosion and run-off problems which will impede public use of the bike trail and use of the park." The board also reported concerns with other developers who had land adjacent to park land, especially on this lakefront stretch west of the Chicago & Northwestern right-of-way conversion north of Michigan Avenue, and worried that "tolerance of any action by developers may put the County's and the public's most valuable and prized park lands at further risk of encroachment."[182] The parks director reported three calls in a month from developers adjacent to park land who wanted a piece of it to expand their footprint.

The Landmark on the Lake issue was settled in what seems like a good solution: "as a compromise for allowing the fill to remain, the developer has agreed in principle to design and implement an access improvement to the bike trail."[183] In 1991, a group called Citizens Allied for Civic Action wondered whether Chai Point, on Prospect Avenue near Ogden Avenue, was encroaching on an entrance into Juneau Park and the bike path. This was referred to committee and does not appear again in the County Board of Supervisors proceedings.

WATERFRONT ENTITIES

Views from the Oak Leaf can be exhilarating when the path meets the waterfront. Milwaukeeans have ample and easy free access to the Lake Michigan shoreline. It's very different from other parts of the country—for example, some New Jersey beaches restrict access and charge each pedestrian as they approach the ocean.

Today, runners and bicyclists choosing the eastern portion of the trail through Veterans and McKinley Parks pass near the Milwaukee Community Sailing Center and the more elite Milwaukee Yacht Club. McKinley Park contains a government pier popular with people who fish and those who seek a great view. A cleaning station awaits those who successfully catch a fish.

The Coast Guard once owned a portion of this land until the county, after determining that the University of Wisconsin–Milwaukee was not interested in collaborating on an environmental center, moved forward to buy it in the

1970s. The Coast Guard had operated a three-story rectangular Prairie-style structure with a prominent five-story tower and a boathouse. It was built between July 1915 and April 1916.[184] It was added to the National Register of Historic Places on August 7, 1989, and was considered a rare example of nonresidential Prairie style. Members of the American Indian Movement became uninvited guests who overstayed their welcome and occupied the building. In part, they used it as a school. The American Indians "demanded, according to the Treaty of Fort Laramie in 1868, that abandoned federal property should revert to the control of the original inhabitants."[185] The building was eventually demolished.

> *Many attempts were made to restore and preserve the historic building. It was even designated a national landmark on the National Register of Historic Places. Unfortunately, all the attempts to save the building fell short and in late March 2008, the Coast Guard station at McKinley Park was demolished. A pavilion now stands in the place where the station was once located.*[186]

The Coast Guard and its predecessors operated from several different buildings along the lakefront, some on today's east side and others on the south side. A serious shipwreck in the fall of 1875 spurred local petitions resulting in construction of a lifesaving station in 1877 at the end of South Pier, near the new mouth of the Milwaukee River known as the "straight cut." By 1886, the lifesaving station had been relocated to Jones Island, which eventually became polluted due to the outflow of the city's sewerage system, spurring efforts to find a new location on the lakefront. In 1915, the Revenue Cutter Service merged with the U.S. Life-Saving Service to form the Coast Guard. Around this same time, the local organization relocated to new lakefront property at today's 1600 North Lincoln Memorial Drive, within the modern Veterans Park. The Coast Guard used the building until 1970. The Coast Guard built a new station at 2420 South Lincoln Memorial Drive in the city of Milwaukee's Bay View neighborhood, which remains in use.[187] It's visible from the South Shore Corridor of the Oak Leaf Trail on East Russell Avenue—at the lakefront, of course!

The trail continues past the site of the former Maitland Field and Municipal Air Marine Terminal. This airport was near today's Discovery World. Its location allowed passengers to easily access the nearby railway station, Lake Front Depot described earlier. That advantage could not overcome narrow runways not aligned correctly with the lake winds; and unstable ground made from landfill containing glass and nails, which punctured plane tires, hindered the airfield's success.[188] Maitland Field was abandoned in 1956, and the land was leased to the army for defense of the city. (An airport expansion proposed by the harbor commission and the city's planning engineer suggested several runways if the nearby Illinois Steel Company site could be purchased and enhanced with landfill.)

NIKE MISSILE SITE

The word *Nike* means "athletic gear" to modern ears, but it once referred to missile defense. During the Cold War, from 1953 to 1979, the U.S. Army built and operated almost three hundred Nike missile sites in the United States. They were line-of-sight anti-aircraft missiles. In Wisconsin, Illinois and Indiana, these sites were intended as the last line of defense against Soviet bombers that might attack steel and industrial production areas. These were part of the Milwaukee Defense Area and then the Chicago-Milwaukee-Gary Defense Area. The army intended to form a defensive ring around the city.

The Maitland Field area housed a Nike site. Other local sites included River Hills; Warnimont Park; Franklin near the Milwaukee County House of Correction; Muskego on Martin Road; Waukesha on Davidson Road; Menomonee Park; and Havenwoods State Forest Nature Preserve. In addition, Lake Park housed a tracking station on a lease to the federal government that ran from May 12, 1955, to April 30, 1972.[189] Only a concrete building remains in Lake Park, because the Nike station was demolished in 1970. Through a twist of fate, Nike sites and bicycle trails are connected in these places where the modern trail passes:

- Lake Park housed a tracking station
- Warnimont housed a missile site
- The former Maitland Field location, now Summerfest, housed a missile site

Along the waterfront, the trail passes Discovery World, and many trail users continue south into Lakeshore State Park. Many continue to the Milwaukee Pier and pass its red lighthouse. Those continuing farther south take a series of city streets toward Milwaukee's South Side.

SHORT-TERM RENTALS

A contractor operated a short-term bike rental from a shack in McKinley Park alongside the lagoon. Riders could enjoy bicycling along the lakefront for a few hours and then return the rental to the same location. It included comfort bikes and tandem bikes and also rented paddleboards for enjoying the lagoon. In later years, pedal-powered wheeled vehicles for four people were also enjoyed by groups at the lakefront. For a time, Segway tours, with individuals on motorized platforms, occasionally passed along downtown portions of the Oak Leaf.

The Program Subcommittee of the City of Milwaukee Bike and Pedestrian Task Force included in its 2009 goals having a bike sharing system in place in Milwaukee. These systems allow rentals of an hour or even a portion of an hour and allow riders to return a bike to a different spot than where they obtained it. They don't have to ride in a circle or loop but can ride a point-to-point trip, similar to a one-way airline ticket. The trend, popular in other parts of the county and world, reached Milwaukee when the nonprofit Bublr bikes opened in 2014. It continues to operate at sites such as Discovery World near the art museum and non-park areas such as sidewalks near the U.S. Bank skyscraper, Milwaukee School of Engineering and University of Wisconsin–Milwaukee. It began in the city of Milwaukee and spread to other municipalities within the county.

Self-serve short-term bicycle rentals are available in all seasons from Bublr. In summer, bikes are also available to rent from staffed kiosks within Veterans Park. In 2018, the company opened a station in Bradford Beach. *Author's collection.*

Bublr strives to prove more transportation options, and its opening expanded recreational biking, too. It allowed people to leave work or school, pay self-serve with a credit card and enjoy a quick ride. They could return the bike to the pickup spot or to another spot operated by Bublr. This extended opportunities to enjoy portions of the Oak Leaf Trail and was funded in part by the Wisconsin Department of Transportation's Congestion Mitigation/Air Quality Program. Bublr was first open only during warmer weather but expanded to year-round operation in 2015.[190] The company offered pay-as-you-go plans or passes such as an eighty-dollar annual pass in 2018.

To further extend the possible combinations throughout the area, Bublr and the Milwaukee County Transit System announced a partnership in January 2018.[191] It made combining a rental with a bus ride more convenient through an RFID sticker on the bus pass. Bublr bike rides can be a good way to experience short sections of the Oak Leaf, especially the major parks near downtown.

Not So Fast

In 1966, the County Board of Supervisors maximized the speed limit in parks and parkways to twenty-five miles per hour with an exception on Lincoln Memorial Drive. The regulation still stands as Milwaukee County Code of Ordinance 47.10(5)(a).[192] This regulation helps make riders and runners comfortable, as most cars pass at a reasonable speed.

Part III

SOUTH SHORE LINE

Cupertino, South Shore, Bay View, Sheridan, Warnimont and Grant Parks

Riders and runners on Milwaukee's south side enjoy one of the oldest sections of the Oak Leaf Trail. It began with an experimental section in Warnimont and Sheridan Parks and eventually expanded and became the South Lakefront bicycle trail, traveling from the parkland east of Russell Avenue through the present Cupertino, South Shore, Bay View, Sheridan, Warnimont and Grant Parks. It crossed exclusively through public parkland with only one exception: the Wisconsin Electric Power Company land in St. Francis.

Along nearly this exact Cupertino–South Shore–Bay View–Sheridan–Warnimont–Grant route, today's trail users embark on a beautiful excursion uninterrupted by cross streets or advertising. Other than a few driveways, the only encumbrances are other athletes and occasional Canada geese or squirrels crossing the path. Foxes and coyotes make occasional appearances. The trail leaves the city streets' grid pattern and slides along Lake Michigan's shore. It gives due attention to the world's fifth-largest lake as it leaves behind the idea of the straightest route from one point to another and becomes attuned to nature's slight curves. This eight-mile section, marked "South Shore Corridor" or "South Shore Line" on some maps, provides a wonderful view of the sunrise, post-work exercise or a spot to glimpse migrating birds or enjoy a woodsy stroll.

A particularly historic portion is in Warnimont and Sheridan Parks, where today's Oak Leaf Trail continues along a short experimental path built in 1968 with a turnaround loop still visible today. (The turnaround seems to appear out of nowhere and has perplexed present-day riders who ponder its purpose.) This trail was about a mile and a half and was partially funded by the Land and Water Conservation Act through the Wisconsin Department of Natural Resources Bureau of Outdoor Recreation.[193]

The South Lakefront bicycle trail became the second trail in the Milwaukee area, preceded by its northern sibling, Lake Park trails, by a year. Funding for both was evenly split between local dollars and Land and Water Conservation Act money.

RUSSELL AVENUE

Before arriving on the blacktop path, riders and runners on the South Shore Corridor going clockwise along the Oak Leaf Trail are heading east on Russell Avenue in Milwaukee's Bay View neighborhood. They can't help noticing the historical sign about the rolling mill on the northeast corner of Russell Avenue and Superior Street. The Wisconsin Historical Society erected the marker in 1985 to explain that the mill produced iron products, including rail for railroads. The sign explains a local tragedy, beginning with this background: "On May 5, 1886, the mill was the scene of a major labor disturbance. Nearly 1500 strikers from around Milwaukee marched on the Bay View mill to dramatize their demand for an eight-hour work day. The local militia, called to the scene by Governor Jeremiah Rusk, fired on the crowd, killing seven people." The rolling mill workers lived on the blocks nearby and helped found churches and organizations like the South Shore Yacht Club. Along with their families, they enjoyed lakefront views just like today's trail users. A small local gathering each year commemorates the shootings and the struggle for fair labor practices. The sign is the only state historical marker on the South Shore Corridor, but other small markers indicate the site of the former power plant or the CCC camp. Many more could be erected to reveal the compelling history of the land and water.

The historical society marker sits on land created by landfill and owned by the City of Milwaukee Harbor Commission. In 2000, developer Leigh Bryan Zarse proposed a twenty-seven-story residential and office building, which was not successful. If it had been built, the entryway to the South Shore Corridor would create a different impression on trail users, who would be traveling between two high-rises rather than between a high-rise and open land.

As trail users continue east on Russell Avenue, they see the tallest building in the area at twenty-five stories. It occupies the southwest corner of Shore Drive and Russell Avenue. The developer would have built it taller, but the Federal Aviation Administration had an air easement due to the traffic headed to nearby Mitchell Field.[194] The restriction seems reasonable, as riders and runners often see and hear planes screaming overhead as they descend toward Michell Field's runways. The building was first occupied in 1964 and was known as Bay View Terrace Apartments, becoming Bay View Terrace Condominium in 1980. It was controversial at first, and many units did not sell as condos and were occupied instead as apartments. On April 11, 1989, a helicopter was lifting 2,500 pounds of air-conditioning equipment to the building's top. A drive shaft coupling failed, and the helicopter crashed, though pilot Ben Moore had no major injuries. Displaying strong Midwest values, he asked to return to finish the job. Riders on the Milwaukee 76 that day may have witnessed quite a scene.

This couple enjoys a walk with their dog as a St. Patrick's Day fun run concludes behind them. Bay View Terrace Condominium is visible in the background. *Author's collection.*

Just north of this location, riders and runners see the current U.S. Coast Guard station at 2420 South Lincoln Memorial Drive. The Coast Guard started using it in 1970. Back in the 1950s and 1960s, two submarines docked in this area—the USS *Tautog* and then the USS *Cobia*.[195] They were important naval ships with success in World War II. The *Cobia* is now in the Wisconsin Maritime Museum in Manitowoc, is a National Historic Landmark and is listed on the National Register of Historic Places. Today, a small gate between the Coast Guard and the nearby Oak Leaf Trail allows access to a long pier extending into the lake. It provides unique maritime views and great perspectives on the downtown skyline, especially at sunrise (and it opens well before sunrise). Visitors walk past the property of the local chapter of the Sea Scouts, an international organization founded by the United Kingdom's Lord Robert Baden-Powell, the same man who founded the Boy Scouts.[196]

HOAN BRIDGE

Looking north from Cupertino Park, runners and riders glimpse a dramatic bridge linking Bay View to downtown. The Hoan Bridge has dominated the skyline west of the port and the Coast Guard area since the 1970s. It was originally named the Harbor Bridge but was renamed to honor former Milwaukee mayor Daniel Hoan. Locals nicknamed it the "Bridge to Nowhere" around its completion in 1972 because it sat vacant (except for an appearance in the movie *The Blues Brothers*). The nearly two-mile-long empty steel bridge ironically won the American Institute of Steel Construction Long Span Bridge Award in 1975. A judge commented, "This is a graceful structure that combines elegance with simplicity. The constant depth of the tie girder and its visual relationship with the arch give a streamlined effect. This is an impressive gateway to Milwaukee's harbor."[197] Traffic finally began flowing across it in 1977, when it was accessible from surface streets. Local freeway projects were very controversial, and planned freeway connections were canceled. The bridge has undergone major repairs but has retained its well-known color combination of mustard yellow and light blue.

Running and bicycling races and rides sometimes cross it, but otherwise the bridge is not open to pedestrians or bicyclists. Some leaders had a much different vision for the bridge. On May 15, 1979, eighteen state legislators representing districts within Milwaukee County requested approval and designation of a bicycle lane on the bridge from Gerald Reihsen, acting division administrator of the Federal Highway Administration in Madison. The county supervisors added their voice, with Daniel Cupertino Jr. from Bay View, Harout Sanasarian from downtown/East Side and R. Michael Mett of Shorewood cosponsoring a resolution. They stated that the Hoan would forge an important linkage in the Milwaukee County bicycle system. The county board petitioned the secretary of the Wisconsin Department of Transportation, the Honorable Lowell Jackson, "to approve of said request and recommend concurrence by the Federal Highway Administration."[198] It never happened, but the idea stuck around.

Thirty years later, the Facilities Subcommittee of the City of Milwaukee Bike and Pedestrian Task Force shared an impressive vision for the bridge, making it bikeable and walkable with scenic overlooks like famous bridges in other cities, such as the Golden Gate Bridge in San Francisco and the Brooklyn Bridge in New York City.[199] Local citizens, advocacy groups and politicians like Patricia Jursik advocated for a way for people to use the Hoan. In a guest editorial in the *Bay View Compass* newspaper, Jursik, then a county supervisor, wrote:

> *The Hoan Bridge already offers visitors driving over the iconic span dramatic, panoramic views of the city skyline and the Milwaukee Art Museum's Santiago Calatrava-designed* Brise Soleil. *We now have the opportunity to extend the privilege of that view to bicyclists and pedestrians, while creating a unique destination that will garner national attention.*
>
> *Why not suspend a bridge cantilevered off the side of the arch of the Hoan? This span would allow both bikers and walkers to ascend 120 feet to take in the unrivaled view of the lake and city.*[200]

The Wisconsin Department of Transportation (WisDOT) did evaluate the feasibility of adding a shared-use path to the bridge as part of a rehabilitation project and shared the results with the public in 2011.[201] It never came to pass. Except for rare special events, only vehicles and seagulls regularly cross the Hoan. The Oak Leaf Trail and predecessor routes going back to at least the Milwaukee 64 have never enjoyed a direct north–south route and rely on a patchwork route with frequent turns on city streets. A section of converted railroad right-of-way that opened in July 2013 between Washington and Maple Streets as an alternative to the bus-laden First Street

The Hoan Bridge connects the south shore and downtown. Despite decades of interest from local politicians advocating for pedestrian and bicycling options, the bridge is dedicated to vehicles except for rare special events. *Jenna Stoll Photography.*

or its next-door neighbor Second Street helped but only addressed a portion of the north–south connection.[202]

Decades ago, urban planners and political leaders envisioned the eventual Lake Parkway being integrated in a much larger Lake Freeway. Fighting the freeway extension was a major issue for local politician Daniel Cupertino Jr. Shortly after taking office on the County Board of Supervisors in 1972, he introduced a resolution to freeze the auctioning of homes in the path of the southern segment of the Lake Freeway. When residents were asked to vote on routes for the freeway display in the courthouse, he took the bold step of adding another option:

> *Models and drawings of alternate designs for the Lake Freeway are on display at the Courthouse. Supervisor Daniel Cupertino of the 17th District has posted a fifth choice alongside other choices. Cupertino urges citizens to vote "My choice: None." This is followed by one main reason, "save the park." The display is in a central corridor of the Courthouse across from Room 306. Thursday, two labor leaders protested against Cupertino's addition. But county officials said they had no intention of removing his sign.*[203]

Daniel Hoan was recognized nationally as an excellent city leader. He is in the front row at right, with New York mayor Fiorello La Guardia next to him. *Library of Congress.*

Despite this bold political side, newspaper articles portray Cupertino as a fun-loving man and so friendly to his fellow residents that he would invite a passing bus driver to stop and have a sausage during a gathering on his front lawn. He said Bay View was more of a feeling than a place on a map and was proud of its character. He is best known for his fight to retain this character and keep the more extensive freeway out. It's difficult to say how a more extensive freeway would have impacted bicycling options. Freeways create barriers for a trail to cross, but their construction can bring funding.

In 1982, the county parks removed lifeguards from South Shore and some other beaches. The Milwaukee 76 bicycle trail passed alongside this beach, and some children rode there with towels over their shoulders to enjoy a refreshing dip. Lifeguards were retained at Bradford, Grant (farther south on the trail) and Doctors Park significantly north. Cupertino tried to get guards restored in his district after seeing large crowds on the beach, especially during holidays. He was unsuccessful but kept trying. In 1978, he submitted but withdrew a proposal to get South Shore a pool like the one in Pulaski Park.[204] If a lifeguarded pool or clean, lifeguarded lakefront beach free of dangerous bacteria had become reality, many more people would likely ride the trail in this part of the county with towels in their backpacks.

During Cupertino's tenure, Milwaukee undertook a massive sewer project nicknamed the "Deep Tunnel." Workers had to dig through bedrock 135 to 300 feet underground to create the tunnel, and the rock had to go somewhere.[205] These tunnel spoils were placed on the South Shore Park shoreline to the St. Francis border in an attempt to stem lakefront erosion. (In a similar way, landfill from the Marquette Interchange would be used to create rolling hills in the Menomonee Valley.[206]) The tunnel spoils were augmented in 2005 as part of a larger project to handle erosion.

After suffering strokes, Cupertino—or "Cup"—died on November 16, 1996. To honor this long-serving south side politician, some leaders considered naming South Shore Park after him. They settled on naming the northern portion in his honor, and Cupertino Park is now the first in a chain of parks along the South Shore Corridor of the Oak Leaf Trail.

Historic postcards show crowds in the water and walking along the beach in approximately the same location as today's Oak Leaf Trail in South Shore Park. It's human nature to walk along a shoreline to enjoy the view. This area was once a popular spot for watery fun and relief from the heat, but it is no longer a popular swimming spot. The swimming beach is currently monitored for bacteria like *Escherichia coli* (E. coli), a perennial problem with runoff and bird droppings polluting the water and the breakwater keeping water trapped along the shore. Large signs display whether it is red (closed), yellow (questionable) or green (clear). For many years, the beach was "red" for consecutive days and even weeks and unfit for swimming. A University of Wisconsin–Milwaukee report explained that "In 2000, closings spanned 60% of the swimming season....At times levels of E. coli were 65 times over the EPA recommended limit (235 CFU/100 ml) for recreational waters."[207] The beach was closed more frequently than any other beach on the Great Lakes.[208] A mix of public and private dollars have improved the area.

- Parks Department staff requested a grant from MillerCoors to help return the water to acceptable swimming levels. The company funded work via a $500,000 grant (distributed over five years at $100,000 per year) via the Park People.[209]
- In 2017, the county finished a $3.7-million green infrastructure improvement project. It partnered with the Milwaukee

Metropolitan Sewerage District (MMSD), the Great Lakes Restoration Initiative (GLRI), the University of Wisconsin–Milwaukee School of Freshwater Science, Wisconsin DNR and the Fund for Lake Michigan.
- To determine future needs, the Environmental Protection Agency granted $350,000 to GLRI. The money went to the Wisconsin DNR and then to Milwaukee County.
- The Park Watch (now Friends of South Shore Park) helped with several water quality projects between 1995 and 2010. With the Great Lakes Water Institute, it started testing the water and cleaning up the beach. A state project involved putting drains at the boat launch. A rain garden was built near the water to see if it prevented runoff from affecting the lake. They teamed up with MMSD to get local residents, especially along nearby Delaware Avenue and surrounding streets, to plant rain gardens and use rain barrels to prevent runoff.

Cleanup efforts like these allowed the beach to more frequently pass tests for bacteria. A major overhaul of the South Shore Yacht Club parking lot in 2017 involved some rerouting of the Oak Leaf and brought it some new surfacing and signage. The $3-million county project improved the parking lot and included three biofiltration areas to help clear up water before it reaches the lake.[210] The new route minimizes the distance riders and runners are in the yacht club parking lot, keeping them more protected on the lakeside perimeter compared to the old route.

In September 2018, contractors hired by Milwaukee County Parks personnel described four options for relocating the beach to provide safer swimming.[211] That year, high bacteria levels caused warning signs to be posted on fifty-seven of the ninety-seven days of the traditional swimming season between Memorial Day and Labor Day.

In the 1970s, the county board looked into entities using county land but not paying rental fees. The South Shore Yacht Club, at 2300 East Knock Street in South Shore Park, had been at the site for decades but wasn't paying a fee to the county. Bay View residents started the club in a rented house on today's South Shore Drive, then moved onto a ramshackle ship they refurbished called the *Lilly E*, which they eventually had to incinerate. They moved a few more times until they got a dedicated clubhouse in 1938. They got a thirty-year lease in 1972 with "a minimum investment of $260,000."[212] An ongoing dispute about property ownership between

Nature lovers enjoy picturesque views near the South Shore Yacht Club. The *Lake Express Ferry* is visible in the center, right. *Jenna Stoll Photography.*

the club and the county was resolved in 2006, with the club acknowledging Milwaukee County ownership and signing a long-term lease.[213]

The club was founded by blue-collar men from nearby mills, forges and factories. It didn't admit women as members until the 1980s, so they participated through a ladies' auxiliary. A junior club began in 1938. That same year, the club began its Queen's Cup race across Lake Michigan with a fabulous, intricate silver trophy made in England in 1847 or 1848.[214] The South Shore Yacht Club website displays the race's date, which in 2018 took place in June. Watching the ships sail into the distance from the Oak Leaf in great weather is a relaxing, picturesque experience. On some weeknights in summer, the white sails of various crews practicing are magnificent against the blue water and sky, so Oak Leaf Trail users pause to take in the view. In 2006, the club spent capital on a major expansion and renovation. (The parking lot and nearby area were part of a different improvement project described earlier in this book.) The group had 479 members at the start of 2018.[215]

FERRY OPTIONS

From the beach and surrounding areas of South Shore Park at the edge of Lake Michigan, a rider or runner looking north overlooks the former Jones Island and the current Port of Milwaukee. Sometimes large ships hove into view or the *Lake Express Ferry* can be seen making its way between Milwaukee and Muskegon, Michigan. When it opened in June 2004, the *Lake Express Ferry* was a return to the past traditions of passenger ships. The SS *Milwaukee Clipper* operated from 1940 to 1970, eventually becoming a National Historic Landmark, and is now on display in Muskegon.[216] Even older ships passed through these waters on regular routes. Charles Whitnall writing in the 1920s pointed out, "For years there were a number of lake boats that carried passengers. The Goodrich two side-wheel boats were the first and the last running to Sheboygan, Milwaukee and Chicago. However, the time came when boat lines were doomed, and minds began to speculate about land travelways."[217]

Some inventive weekend warriors combine the Oak Leaf Trail with the *Lake Express Ferry*. The ferry dock is a very short ride from this area of the Oak Leaf, and bicyclists and walkers can purchase tickets to come aboard. Some locals stock their bicycles with camping gear, ride the Oak Leaf and a local street to the ferry departure, board the ferry and spend about two and a half hours crossing Lake Michigan to Muskegon.

Jake Newborn has enjoyed several camping trips via bicycle. In 2017, he and his wife, Nicole La Brie, and daughter July took three trips. The family joined with some friends and took the *Lake Express Ferry* to Muskegon, Michigan, then rode about eight miles to P.J. Hoffmaster State Park. Of course they reversed the process to get home and got to tell the tale of their land-sea-camping adventure. On another outing, Newborn and his family rode the Oak Leaf Trail south to the Wulff Lodge in Grant Park with a group from the Coast Inn bicycle shop. Their third trip was via the Oak Leaf Trail north to the Interurban and up to Harrington Beach State Park in Belgium, Wisconsin, about forty-five miles each way. Newborn rode a Bulitt cargo bike, and La Brie rode a road bike with their young daughter as passenger.[218]

At Russell Avenue's eastern end, trail users can take for granted the small path that takes them from the road toward the water. But in the early 1970s, this was considered a treacherous area, because no path existed down the steep hill:

Milwaukee County's Oak Leaf Trail

> *The Park Commission recommends participation with the City of Milwaukee in developing the pedestrian walkway.... The county board approves spending $7,000 as a proportionate share of the planning, engineering and construction costs with the City of Milwaukee picking up the other portion since this area is a flushing tunnel site.*[219]

The path provided a safe way to get down to the lakefront with a particularly picturesque view of downtown. Eventually, this same spot was part of the Milwaukee 76 and became the entryway to the South Shore Corridor of the Oak Leaf Trail. Its short but steep grade—one of the steeper hills on this part of the route—makes it still something to be reckoned with. At its base in the park, many amateur athletes have paused to admire the view east over Lake Michigan and north to the high-rises of downtown. They may have wondered about a circular pattern that is often assumed to be a helicopter landing pad. In reality, this is the much less interesting flushing tunnel, in place since at least the 1970s.

For many years, the Bay View Bicycle Club sponsored a sign posted on this hill with a map. Bay View business owner and bicyclist Dick Knepper founded the club in 1989. Group members ride not only in the Milwaukee area but also the surrounding counties every weekend between April and October. Their website, bayviewbikeclub.org, includes: "At the BVBC, we promote bicycling not only for its overall health benefits, but just as importantly for the opportunity to meet diverse people, create friendships, share our riding experiences as well as everyday experiences and enjoy the camaraderie of fellow bicyclists. We do it because we enjoy people and bicycles."

Most of the off-road portions of the Oak Leaf Trail are converted rail lines or former farmland that became parkland. The South Shore section does not contain converted railroad rights-of-way, so these riders are proceeding through former farmland. In particular, the land of today's South Shore Park was part of the farm of Elijah Stone Estes. An east–west street is

A rider on the south side reviews his map or cue sheet during the early days of the Milwaukee 76 bicycle trail. *Milwaukee County Parks.*

named Estes and ends a bit north of the South Shore pavilion. Back in 1912, South Shore Park was enhanced with a bathhouse. In 1933, Depression-era relief workers improved the park and erected the pavilion, designed by the prominent Milwaukee architectural firm Ferry and Clas (sometimes called Clas & Clas). (The firm also created the Milwaukee Public Library, known today as Central Library, and its design for that structure beat out over seventy competitors, including Frank Lloyd Wright.)

The firm would likely be proud of the popularity of its South Shore pavilion, which remains in demand for weddings, reunions, *quinceañeras* (fifteenth birthday parties) and more. It fills with celebrations almost every Friday and Saturday night in summer and fall with music often spilling out onto the trail and park. It also serves as a voting site. A farmer's market on summer Saturdays brings a crowd to its doorstep. Runners often stop and refuel at the market with a muffin and coffee.

In warm weather, riders and runners pass a busy beer garden staffed by county parks personnel. This is a mostly outdoor facility partially enclosed by walls of the pavilion. It's a great stopping point for a bathroom break

South Shore Park's pavilion is a convenient spot to use the bathroom and water fountain. It's rented by groups many evenings and weekends and hosts a popular beer garden in warm months. *Author's collection.*

Sections of the trail that are free of cars give children a bit of freedom (though they still have to watch out for bicyclists). *Author's collection.*

and beer or other beverage. The beer garden has restrooms on the lake side, or runners and walkers can often access the restrooms at the western side of the building, away from the lake. The nearby playground previously bore a marker naming it Harnischfeger, after the company that formerly had a headquarters to the south and gave the largest donation for the playground's construction.

For decades, the South Shore Park pavilion stood near the epicenter of an epic party: South Shore Water Frolic. The event started in 1948 or 1949. According to Ron Winkler in his book *Bay View*, the Frolic evolved from the South Shore Yacht Club's Hi-Jinks event.[220] Ambitious organizers from the Inter-Organizational Council of Bay View likely did not dream that they were starting an event that would continue for sixty-eight years and draw two hundred thousand at its peak.[221] Events took place on land and in the water. The weekend event evolved with the times and drew smaller but substantial crowds of thirty to forty thousand per day, with totals of seventy thousand visitors over the weekend, many who once lived in Bay View or came from nearby areas to enjoy a festival with no entry fee. Local companies, including bars, sponsored girls in a beauty contest. Bicycle riders had to deal with temporary trail closures before and during the festival by detouring a short distance.

In the 2000s, the event involved evening fireworks and stages with bands and a parade with the usual classic cars, local politicians and media personalities, plus floats and local groups like the Daley Debutantes baton twirlers. The quirky character of Bay View shone through when some years, inexplicably, a person in a chicken headdress played drums with a band. Organizers dropped the reference to water in its name and added an "s" to become the South Shore Frolics. It gradually earned less for its nonprofit organizers and drew fewer partiers and more neighborhood complaints, especially over the noise of fireworks. The modern organizers, the Lions Club, could no longer find parade sponsors, and in 2017, they suspended the whole event for 2018 and indefinitely thereafter.

After passing the South Shore Park pavilion, riders or runners continuing south on the Oak Leaf Trail reach a fork in the path. They can choose to stay along the lakefront, which was badly eroded in the late 1990s and eventually repaired, or they can go up the bluff and pass scenic homes. In 1976, the county made sure the upper path was viable and arranged a land swap for a thirty-by-one-hundred-foot strip with Lauris and Dorothy Schuette in exchange for a triangular parcel of approximately the same size between their home and South Superior Street.[222]

The path along the lakefront at the base of the bluff was precious to many riders and runners, who enjoyed hearing small waves hit the shore and birds soar overhead. Some stopped to hunt sea glass along the beach. But the path was totally washed out in the late 1990s, and users were unable to continue along this route, being forced to go a bit inland and follow city streets. The South Shore breakwater was in bad shape, too. Locals worried about the amount of traffic coming through the park during morning rush hour and duck hunters shooting in the area. In March 1996, they held the first Park Watch meeting at South Shore Park to work on issues like these.

Eventually, the breakwater was repaired, large boulders were placed along the shoreline to help prevent erosion, and the bike trail was repaved along the shoreline. A 10-foot-wide asphalt path extending 5,200 feet along Lake Michigan, reconnecting South Shore Park and Bay View Park, opened in October 2005. A promotion flyer for the opening stated:

> *The realignment of this trail segment, along with the shoreline protection work, will help eliminate past wash outs and erosion issues. The new*

Erosion encroached on these popular stairs to the beach in Bay View Park. *Bay View Historical Society/Kathy Mulvey.*

Wave action destroyed part of the Oak Leaf trail in the South Shore Corridor. This section was eventually rebuilt. *Bay View Historical Society/Kathy Mulvey.*

paved trail will allow bikers, walkers, runners, strollers, wheel chairs, etc, increased access to Milwaukee's lakefront.

The South Shore Bike Trail significantly adds to the Milwaukee County Park System's overall goal of completing the Oak Leaf Trail and increasing off-road mileage. This project, along with the St. Francis and Drexel Avenue to Loomis Avenue segments, add to this vision of increased connectivity and safety.[223]

In 2015, automatic trail counters captured the traffic along the trail in front of the Texas Avenue extension at the Texas Avenue Pumping Station. In August, they captured 24,180 users on the trail using an automated counter called a "pyro box." The daily average was 780, and the busiest days were Saturday, August 22, 2015 (1,490), Saturday August 1, 2015 (1,175) and Monday, August 3, 2015 (1,058). The busiest window was from 10:00 a.m. to noon.[224]

Riders and runners on the more inland part of the path cross the eastern end of Oklahoma Avenue. Here they could connect with a bus line, since Milwaukee County Transit System (MCTS) vehicles have had bike racks since 2009. The Bicycle Federation of Wisconsin had been advocating for racks for several years.[225] Prior to that, bikes were allowed onboard, but hauling a bike into the bus was cumbersome. The project cost $405,000 ($384,750 from a federal grant and $20,000 from MCTS). Most bus rack users are commuters on a regular routine, but inventive athletes can access new parts of the Oak Leaf Trail by combining a bike ride with a bus route. The bus racks are especially helpful for people who don't own a vehicle or who have a vehicle but no bike rack of their own.

A rider loads a bicycle onto a county bus rack. *Milwaukee County Transit System.*

BAY VIEW PARK

South of Oklahoma Avenue, the trail passes beautiful parkland with no amenities except a water fountain and set of stairs to the lake. Portions of its trail were constructed fairly early, as indicated in a 1973 cue sheet for the Milwaukee 64 ride. That ride's instructions indicate that a .8-mile bike path was available. Riders went west on Texas Avenue, took Superior Street for .1 mile and rode the .8-mile path until returning to Superior Street.

Before white settlers reached the area, this land is thought to have been a summer camp for the Deer Creek Indians, who took advantage of the plentiful animals and fish. Arrowheads and other artifacts indicate they were Potawatomi. They left after the 1833 Treaty of Chicago.[226]

This simple park, Bay View, has grand views of the trees and water and a set of religiously affiliated buildings on its western section. They belong to the Sisters of St. Francis of Assisi, the St. Francis de Sales Seminary and the Catholic Archdiocese of Milwaukee (called the Cousin's Center). St. Mary's Academy was an impressive cream city brick building used as a girls' high school beginning in 1904 and later as nonprofit offices. The building and memories meant so much to some graduates that they stopped by and literally hugged the building before it was dismantled in 2017. Housing for nuns was constructed at the site.[227] Many locals hike or walk dogs through the solitude of Seminary Woods southwest of the seminary buildings, though it isn't official parkland and isn't on the Oak Leaf route.[228] It also isn't easy to find since it lacks signage. Those who find it are rewarded with solitude and a deep sense of escape to untouched forest with informal walking paths among American beech, basswood and sugar maples. Among its sublime trees, time seems to slow down and perspectives begin to shift.

Just across the Milwaukee city border in St. Francis, at 3600 South Lake Drive was WEPCo land. The Lakeside Power Plant began operation in 1920 and became "the world's largest plant to exclusively burn pulverized coal. The lighted smokestacks were visible to ship captains and airplane pilots for miles off shore until 1987 when the plant was razed."[229] At one time, this was the only interruption in parkland for the eight miles of the South Shore Corridor. Riders had to detour onto public streets across the 1.3 miles of lakefront the power company owned. Eventually, the county obtained an easement to allow riders to cross the land and paid a little extra for insurance so the power company would be held harmless for any potential accidents on the land.[230] The trail's move from the St.

Francis streets onto the power company's land provided a safer and more picturesque path for riders. Tracks at a rail line were paved over.[231]

When WEPCo closed the Lakeside Power Plant, the county considered purchasing the land. Its acquisition would provide parkland along the whole stretch from South Shore Park to Grant Park. However, the county didn't have the funds. County supervisor Daniel Cupertino reflected, "It wasn't only the money to buy it, but we would also have to spend millions to clean up asbestos and fly-ash contamination and protect the shoreline from erosion." Speaking to a reporter in the 1990s, he clearly had deep regret. "Fifty years from now, our great-grandchildren will probably condemn us. They'll ask how we could possibly have allowed that land to be developed," he lamented.[232]

The land transferred from the power company to Harnischfeger Corporation, and the bike trail was rerouted closer to the road to avoid a planned underground parking ramp. In 2002, Stark Investments moved in. In 2008, Stark announced plans to spend $35 million expanding but then retreated and moved out of St. Francis.[233] The building underwent reinforcements to its exterior glass, fences and parking lot to become part of the Federal Bureau of Investigation. Trail users pass what must be the most fortified building along the Oak Leaf and ride, walk or run between the building's imposing fence and Lake Drive. Nearby, a large private condominium tower also allows public access for the bicycle trail. In the summer of 2018, the St. Francis Historical Society erected a historical marker along the Oak Leaf Trail with a photograph and description of the plant. A new 214-unit apartment building was under construction at 4000 South Lake Drive by Bear Development LLC. Atlanta-based Campbell Capital proposed a nearby project that fall, specifically citing the location along the Oak Leaf as one of the desirable features.[234]

Northwest of this area is land used for hiking and skiing, marked occasionally with signs as the Nojoshing Trail. (Nojoshing, according to the St. Francis Historical Society, is a Native American word for "straight tongue," referring to land protruding out into Lake Michigan like a straight tongue.[235]) Some people walking in the area connect an outing on the Nojoshing with Seminary Woods and the Oak Leaf Trail.

Large buildings at the Landing condominiums at Park Shore require riders to choose a steep hill with glorious views of Lake Michigan or a flat route along the sidewalk. Running up it is a good way to increase the heart rate. Bicycling up it requires one of the few gear changes on the South Shore Corridor. (Bicycling down gives a thrilling boost of speed.) Farther south, past Warnimont's Kelly Senior Center, the path crosses the driveway for Lakeshore Towers apartments, so riders have to stay aware but aren't too far removed from their immersion in nature.

SHERIDAN PARK

After passing the large condominiums at the Landing, riders and runners going south on the Oak Leaf enjoy parkland on the lakefront and private homes to the west. This is one of the few stretches of the South Shore Corridor that passes private homes. Trail users continuing through Sheridan Park see a softball/baseball field and statue that they might expect is Civil War hero Phillip Sheridan, the park's namesake. Instead, the prominent statue honors Patrick Cudahy, owner of a large, successful meatpacking company. The whole park once bore his name—after all, he graciously sold forty acres of beautiful bluffs and lakefront property that became the park at half price. In 1892, Cudahy bought an enormous amount of land—seven hundred acres—in the city that would later be named in his honor. Modern-day Cudahy was formerly called Buckhorn and then the town of Lake. The area's appeal included being the highest elevation of lakefront land between Milwaukee and Chicago and easy access to the Chicago & Northwestern rail line.[236]

In other parts of the Oak Leaf Trail, railroad track such as former Chicago & Northwestern right-of-way was converted to trail. Here, the rail-to-trail connection is more nebulous but still crucial. The rail helped make the Buckhorn land valuable to Cudahy, who purchased it with his brother John as silent partner and eventually sold thirty valuable acres of lakefront property for public use. His generosity included donating half of the purchase price, so he collected $500 per acre financed at 5 percent rather than $1,000 per acre.[237] The land of today's Sheridan Park once included a summer home for orphans at 4832 South Lake Drive called St. Ann's Home, renamed St. Vincent's Summer Home. The Oak Leaf Trail passes through this general area near Sheridan Park's tennis courts and swimming pool. Cudahy made significant contributions to the public's enjoyment of the South Shore Corridor, because he also provided an interest-free loan to acquire much of the land that became Grant Park. He served on the Milwaukee County Park Commission from its inception in 1907 until his death in 1919 and had a love of plants, including roses.[238]

> ## Wireless Radio
>
> At a time when most of the country didn't even have electricity, Warren Johnson and Charles Fortier experimented with a 150-foot-high radio tower in today's Sheridan Park. They took advantage of the land's remarkable elevation and successfully sent radio signals to and from Racine until their steel tower was destroyed by bad weather, twice! Johnson would become well-known as the founder of the Johnson Controls company. A small marker indicates the spot for posterity.[239]

Cudahy's planning commission purchased more land to extend the park in 1925 (an additional 25 acres) and again in 1928 (an additional 7 acres), then transferred the park to the county in 1931. The park at this time was 66.25 acres.[240] The park shrank a little in April 1964, when the City of Cudahy swapped with Milwaukee County for land to build Cudahy Senior High School. The Oak Leaf Trail passes east of the high school on the bluff above Lake Michigan.

The Oak Leaf Trail in Sheridan Park passes a pond that was once a somewhat muddy swimming spot and winter ice skating area. Continuing on, the trail passes an outdoor pool built by Works Progress Administration labor and improved in 1989–1990.[241] Happy noises from children playing during summer lift the spirits of today's riders. The pool's water fountain, painted to resemble a red mushroom, was added in the 1990s; it is imprinted on the minds of many area children and brings a smile to passersby.

The Sheridan Park pool was the starting point of the second off-road bicycle trail in Milwaukee County. The trail opened in 1968, started at the eastern side of the pool and wove gracefully through the park, past the golf course and to a turnaround loop south of Ramsey Avenue and South Lake Drive between Henry Avenue and Klieforth Avenue. The turnaround point is still visible today to runners and riders and on satellite imagery such as Google Maps. It was eight feet wide and paved asphalt. Funding from the Land and Water Conservation Act contributed $9,000 of the total cost of $18,000. Despite it being designated as a bicycle trail, nearby groups including Cudahy High School teams used it for cross-country training.

A 1972 County Park Commission report stated, "It is obvious to anyone riding these trails that they are very popular and well used. This in itself should indicate more of the same type of facility for future development."[242] This was one of the earliest sections of what would eventually become the Milwaukee 76. Bicyclists got to enjoy a longer path after a December 1972 approval of an 8.8-mile extension. Planners considered two routing options and then gave the go-ahead:

> *WHEREAS, the system of bicycle trails in the Milwaukee County parks has received national recognition; and,*
> *WHEREAS, this helpful sport should be expanded as much as possible by adding additional trails; and,*
> *WHEREAS, the County Park Commission has submitted a report for two routes which would extend the said trails; and,*
> *WHEREAS, the alternate route consisting of 8.8 miles of bikeways is deemed the safer of the two routes; now, therefore*
> *BE IT RESOLVED, that the report from the County Park Commission be approved in principle; and,*
> *BE IT FURTHER RESOLVED, that the safer route, consisting of 8.8 miles of bikeways be approved.*[243]

This segment was lengthened and opened in May 1975. Students involved with the Youth Advisory Bikeway Committee obtained over two thousand signatures supporting a bikeway. On May 18, 1975, riders took a "bike hike" along the trail from the Sheridan Park Clubhouse to Ramsey Avenue, and some riders continued to Grant Park. There, Wisconsin Wheelmen held races.[244]

Locals who were children in the 1970s remember riding the Milwaukee 76 to the Sheridan Park pool and spending a large chunk of the day there, enjoying freedom typically not granted to children in later decades. It was—and continues to be—a great place to cool off under the watch of lifeguards and in temperatures more moderate than the chilly Lake Michigan. Today's park also includes tennis courts and a playground. The field south of the lagoon once used by the semipro Orioles football team is long gone, as are a pavilion and bandshell.

Following World War II, several Milwaukee County parks housed returning veterans to aid in alleviating the housing shortage. Sheridan Park housed a trailer park for them. The park added the Cudahy War Memorial, easily visible from the Oak Leaf Trail, in 1990 at Layton Avenue's eastern end.

South Shore Line

Riders in the late 1960s pause on what is today's South Shore Line of the Oak Leaf Trail. Several are riding tandem bicycles. Safety helmets were not commonly worn. *Courtesy of the Local History Collection of the Cudahy Family Library, Cudahy, Wisconsin.*

Bike riders enjoy a ride on the south side. Young trees in the background are now mature. *Courtesy of the Local History Collection of the Cudahy Family Library, Cudahy, Wisconsin.*

CIVILIAN CONSERVATION CORPS AND WARNIMONT PARK

Citizens enjoying area parks benefitted from the labor of Depression-era relief workers who completed projects like the South Shore Park pavilion. A sign just south of Morris Avenue at South Lake Drive indicates that a Civilian Conservation Corps (CCC) camp operated here between 1933 and 1942 as Company 1644. The corps hired unmarried young men to do things like develop natural resources while earning room and board and some wages. A large chunk of the wages had to be sent home to help workers' families. In Sheridan Park, CCC workers created the service road that leads from the Oak Leaf down the bluff to the water in a snaking pattern. They used that road to haul down huge concrete forms to aid in creating jetties to limit erosion from Lake Michigan waves. They made eleven jetties, each two hundred feet long. Their work lives on, and Oak Leaf Trail riders can

This aerial photograph taken before the bicycling trail was created shows Sheridan Park's jetties and demonstrates how much of the lakefront in this area is reserved for public use via county parks. *Milwaukee County Parks Department.*

carefully access the snaking trail down to the beach, which is otherwise inaccessible in this park and treacherous in its neighbor, Warnimont Park.

Warnimont Park's name helps locals remember Eugene Warnimont, a county supervisor for an impressive thirty-five years who also chaired the board. In addition to the Oak Leaf Trail, its features include a par-three, eighteen-hole golf course, a senior center and a dog exercise area. The area around Kelly Senior Center is particularly good for birdwatching. The forked Aster Hiking Trail is accessible directly from the Oak Leaf but easy to miss because it is signified only with small signs close to the ground. Within Warnimont Park, most people don't know that they are riding or running past the only alkaline wetlands, known as fens, in the area. The fen became a state natural area in 2002 and is owned by Milwaukee County:

> *Numerous groundwater rivulets run down the bluffs and into Lake Michigan and some of the larger rivulets have carved larger, micro gorges into the bluff. The moist, seeping bluffs support a variety of fen plants of considerable botanical interest including grass-of-Parnassus, lesser fringed gentian, Ohio goldenrod, swamp lousewort, and Kalm's lobelia. Other species include soapberry, elk and brittle-leaf sedge, field horsetail, and numerous rushes. Also present is white cedar, here at the southern limit of its range in Wisconsin.*[245]

CUDAHY GUN CLUB

Today's Oak Leaf Trail runners and riders are hard pressed to find any trace of one of the more unusual aspects once alongside the trail: the Cudahy Gun Club. The club began in 1932, and some say that park personnel always had a longstanding rift with it. Shooting and bicycles are not a match made in heaven, and dusty historical records do include official reference to disagreements. One spat concerned the platting of the future Oak Leaf Trail directly alongside the club's territory in Grant Park, which faced out toward the water just north of the golf clubhouse. The County Board of Supervisors proceedings include:

> *The Park Commission is currently engaged in installing a bicycle path in the immediate vicinity of the grounds used for said club....This new construction of the proposed path traverses the parking lot of said club and*

would in a very material way affect the operation of said club….
BE IT RESOLVED, that the County Board of Supervisors assembled this 28th day of May, 1968, request that the Park Commission to cease and desist of all construction immediately interfering with the Cudahy Gun Club facilities, or in the alternative revise their plans for the construction of the bicycle path in such an area approximately 70 feet away that would not interfere with the activities of the Cudahy Gun Club, and
BE IT FURTHER RESOLVED, that the present construction of the bicycle path could well be located in another area of the ground to-wit 70 feet away, and the members of the Gun Club and their guests are ready, willing and able to testify at a time and place set for public hearing by the commission to justify this alternative.[246]

The plea was unsuccessful, and the trail went right past shooters, whose plastic shotgun shells fell along the bluff and even into the water below, washing up on the beach. Nonprofit groups collected piles of them during cleanup efforts. The county board had already threatened to remove the organization by passing a resolution calling for eviction by December 31, 1974, but later rescinded the action. Squabbles continued for decades until the club closed by December 31, 2014, and trail users' enjoyment of nature was no longer peppered with the sound of gunshots.[247] An archery range near the same area never drew much comment and remains open. Its shooters aim arrows at straw bales and do not cause noise or leave behind any plastic.

WARNIMONT NIKE MISSILE SITE

The Oak Leaf Trail in Warnimont Park passes just behind an air missile defense site used from 1956 to 1961 at 6100 South Lake Drive.[248] Tom Brandstetter is a weekend bicyclist who grew up near the site and remembers training on the bicycle path in its early days:

When we were training for cross-country or track, we would run on the new trail. Back then it didn't go all the way to Grant Park. It ended with a small loop a few hundred yards north from Grant.

This loop was on the grounds of the recently decommissioned Nike site. The Nike missile site, seen through the eyes of a young boy, was a big draw.

The Cold War was up close and personal back then. The adults had a better understanding of all the horrors of nuclear war. The kids were scared as well, but knowing there was missile site close to home was sure to bring us to the site to stare through the chain-link fence. For a short period when the missiles were removed and the silos were not yet filled in, the older boys used this as a place for adventure. I was in middle school so didn't have the guts (or was welcomed) to jump the fence and have a few beers with the older boys after climbing down into the silos.[249]

The federal government moved out in 1973, leaving behind a few buildings. The county board appropriated $167,400 and estimated that $100,000 would be needed for annual maintenance. Their proceedings reflect:

WHEREAS, the existing U.S. government constructed "Nike" site buildings located in Warnimont Park are available for county use; and, WHEREAS, the study indicates that the remodeling of and redevelopment of these buildings and adjacent site is a feasible and desirable solution to the needs of the senior citizens as well as youth groups in this portion of the county…
BE IT RESOLVED, that the County Board approves, in principle, the Park Commission recommendation to remodel and redevelop certain of the former "Nike" site buildings located in Warnimont Park for the purposes of senior citizen and youth group recreational activities.[250]

The Warnimont location is far from military now; instead, it's a peaceful site that houses a senior meal program serving free, nutritious hot lunches to seniors over the age of sixty. The nonprofit Interfaith operates a senior center for those over fifty. Younger folks drive past to park their cars and release eager dogs ready for fun at the Warnimont Dog Exercise Area. A few people access the trail, which is visible east of the parking lot.

GRANT PARK

If the Oak Leaf Trail were superimposed onto a clock, Grant Park would sit at about five o'clock. Grant is one of the big, majestic parks right along the lakefront, and the clubhouse has a South Milwaukee address. Grant is also one of the parks not named for a local person or geographic feature.

After debating a nod to President Woodrow Wilson, the commission agreed on the less-controversial Grant.[251] It is the second-largest park in the system. It boasts Lake Michigan swimming with a snack bar, picnicking and golf, along with the famous Seven Bridges Trail for casual hiking. The picturesque trail is always full of people taking photographs. It has beautiful steps alongside trickling water and is a good all-ages hike ending at the lake. The first bridge after the parking lot is inscribed with "Enter this wild wood and view the haunts of nature" and, on the reverse, references to the "peace of this leafy solitude."

Frederick C. Wulff, the first superintendent of horticulture for the parks in the early 1900s, planted trees in this park. He designed the plantings to reflect the Black Forest of Germany and evoke an old-country atmosphere. Grant Park is said to have the only soil in the county comparable with that of northern Wisconsin.[252] In addition to the majestic trees that shelter wildlife like deer, Grant Park boasts amazing views and some attractions made by humans: high on the bluff, the Grant Park pavilion is bedecked with quaint hand-carved figureheads. Each one is unique, and most bring a smile to their observers. A 1960s journalist wrote, "Park officials do not know who did the carvings, but old timers say they predate World War I."[253] The park once included a campground used by tourists driving automobiles, including those following the Yellowstone Trail across the country to the national park or one of the coasts. At its peak in 1929, the camp in Grant Park Tourist Camp registered over 2,500 guests.[254]

GRANT GOLFING

After passing the former gun club site, bikers and runners zoom past the Warnimont Park Golf Clubhouse, which is a convenient stop during the golf season. Riders continue toward Grant Park, where well-established trees and occasional deer provide the most natural part of the South Shore Line.

Most local golfers have enjoyed Grant Park Golf Course at least once. George Hansen designed it, and Milwaukee County's tradition of excellent public courses began when it opened as the county's first public regulation-size course in 1919. Lake Park had already opened a course, but its holes were smaller than typical. The private Michiwaukee Golf Club opened in 1920 with a golf course and clubhouse on Fairy Chasm Road in Bayside, changed its name to North Shore Country Club in 1935 and moved in 1964

> ### Seven Bridges Trail
>
> The beloved Seven Bridges Trail, just off the Oak Leaf in Grant Park, is the site of many short hikes and photo sessions. Its charming paths lead to a natural Lake Michigan beach. It is the result of several major rounds of work and improvement.
>
> - The paths that became Seven Bridges started under Wulff. Designers intentionally followed natural contours rather than ruler-straight lines, in keeping with the philosophy espoused by Charles Whitnall.
> - A crew of two hundred improved it through the 1930s Works Progress Administration.
> - In the 1990s, a much smaller crew made repairs via the Wisconsin Conservation Corps.
>
> A lodge within the park is named after Wulff and hosts youth groups for overnight trips.
>
>
>
> A woman poses near a park amenity—a water fountain, colloquially known as a "bubbler"—near Seven Bridges in Grant Park. The iconic inscribed bridge in the background is the site of many modern photographs. *Milwaukee County Historical Society.*

to Bayside.[255] Grant is regulation size with eighteen holes but, at par three and four, a little shorter than many courses. It was immediately popular, and Charles Whitnall advocated for more holes right away, suggesting another nine "as requested by the golf enthusiasts" in his 1920 parks report. The course was a revenue generator for the park, and Whitnall estimated it would contribute $1,500 to the 1921 budget, a decent amount in its day.

What is now the dramatic yellow clubhouse along the trail was built in 1892 as an impressive Victorian-style private residence for Horace Nathan

Fowle and his wife and nine children. The Fowle family sold their land to the Milwaukee County Parks, and local business owner Patrick Cudahy helped the county with an interest-free loan. Horace Nathan's father, John Fowle, emigrated from England, farmed the area and dammed Oak Creek in 1840. The dam powered first a gristmill and then a sawmill. In 1978, the Milwaukee County Historical Society and Milwaukee County Landmarks Commission designated it an official landmark.

The Oak Leaf Trail goes right past the clubhouse, and trail users can buy a refreshment and use the restroom during golf season. The Fowle family could not have imagined their home becoming a popular golf clubhouse or that the clubhouse would later become a stopping point for golfers, trail runners and riders. Over the years, the clubhouse has offered different meals, serving breakfast in the 1970s and now serving snacks and Friday fish fries during summer. The breakfast was a stopping point for some groups who rode the entire Milwaukee 76 in a single day. Down a steep hill, the beach offers restrooms and a snack shop operated in 2018 by Ferch's.

The huge park was a strategic purchase by the county and ensured a beautiful area was preserved for public use. The shoreline and waterways were protected as part of county ownership. The park, now about 381 acres with additions to the original purchase of Fowle land, has a variety of trees and some say its beauty reminds them of Door County, Wisconsin.[256]

The area wasn't always peaceful, as bikers of another sort—motorcyclists—used it as a gang hangout in the 1970s. "Rowdy types who drank, smoked marijuana and used other drugs frequented the park. The presence of these types intimidated those bicycling, walking and using the park for family activities," described William Redding, then South Milwaukee police chief, in 1982.[257] Regular patrols by plainclothes officers successfully chased away the gangs.

Many people are surprised to learn that Grant Park's women's golf club began in 1934, making it the longest standing women's club in the country. The club made it through wars, social unrest, recessions and the women's rights movement. Some players continued memberships for as long as sixty years. Scott Walker commemorated the club with a proclamation when he was Milwaukee County executive. It's another tradition of fun and athleticism along the Oak Leaf.

In the 1970s, the County Board of Supervisors directed the staff of the park commission to study the creation of a bike trail "from approximately Howell Avenue into Grant Park." The vision was an "exclusive bike trail within the vicinity of Oak Creek"[258] and implies an off-road trail. The full

Grant Park's remarkable golf clubhouse was once a private home. *Milwaukee County Historical Society.*

trail does not appear to have been completed. Modern riders traversing this route east of Howell Avenue rely on Drexel Road, then a paved trail following the Oak Creek Parkway crossing into the city of South Milwaukee and then the parkway itself as they approach the southern end of Grant Park. An old, narrow asphalt path does snake along this part of the parkway.

By about 2010, rough riding afflicted part of the Oak Leaf Trail within Grant Park: patches had uneven or sunken grade, heaved pavement, bumps, cracks, narrowing from adjacent greenery's overgrowth and the occasional gnarly pothole. Some riders chose to travel Lake Drive instead of dealing with the rough conditions. The trail and other parts of the park got improvements in 2015. "Across Milwaukee County we are improving parks and public spaces. From fixing up the long-neglected Oak Leaf Trail in the South Shore to my Urban Parks initiative that has improved parks in the central city, I am committed to continuing to make a difference," said County Executive Chris Abele.[259] Abele's 2015 budget included money for the improvement, which was supported by the county board and Supervisor Patricia Jursik, a longtime bicycling advocate who regularly held rides through the park and advocated for improvements while in office.

After preliminary work such as tree surveying and certifying, about five miles of the trail were widened and improved according to Wisconsin Bicycle Facility Design Handbook standards. The work included two sections:

- Beginning east of Lunham Street near the St. Francis border and continuing through Sheridan Park to Warnimont Park—work by Poblocki Paving Corporation for $350,000
- Beginning at the College Avenue extension and continuing south a short distance, plus a large portion beginning at Park Avenue (in Cudahy) and continuing to the Grant clubhouse, including some rerouting—work by Payne & Dolan for over $800,000

The improvements included widening the trail to ten feet from seven to eight feet. This increased safety by allowing easier passing and more warning of oncoming traffic or even an attacker coming from the nearby bushes or trees.

SOUTH MILWAUKEE YACHT CLUB

This yacht club at 101 Marshall Avenue in South Milwaukee lies just south of Grant Park. Riders taking a break at the lakefront easily spot it. The club incorporated in 1950, and members constructed a clubhouse two years later, then rebuilt the hall in 1989. The group continued improving with a new pavilion, a fish cleaning station in 2006 and a lift allowing easier launch and storage in 2010. At the start of 2018, the club had 263 memberships, and the members ventured beyond boating into card playing (including the local game of sheepshead) and dancing and operated as a co-operative.[260]

Boats on the horizon provide a picturesque view from the Oak Leaf Trail. From this area, riders and runners traveling clockwise leave the lakefront and continue northwest on the Oak Creek Parkway. They fill their lungs with fresh air in the parkways for which Charles Whitnall advocated.

> ## Quick Facts
>
> The Oak Leaf Trail is open 365 days per year during park hours, typically from daylight until 10:00 p.m.
>
> Off-road parts of the trail are constructed of three and a half inches of asphalt with a gravel subbase.

"MEET ME ON THE OAK LEAF"

Song lyrics by John Stano
www.johnstano.com

Our special place is a public space, it's one hundred eight miles long.
It runs by rivers and the lake, through parks and right through the wild
   bird's song,
spring's bight trilliums, summer's fireflies,
you can scrape through the leaves in the fall,
make fresh footprints in winter snow and you can do it all...

Chorus:
...on the Oak Leaf, meet me on the Oak Leaf.
You can run, you can shuffle, you can walk, you can roller blade
take a bike, take a break, you can just stand there.

Our special place is a public space, about twelve feet wide
except when it runs on city streets, then you keep off to the side.
Through the dog days of summer or underneath a cold winter moon
we've been spending too much time indoors, let's get out there soon.

Chorus:
Meet me on the Oak Leaf, meet me on the Oak Leaf.
You can run, you can shuffle, you can walk, you can roller blade
take a bike, take a break, you can just stand there.

"Meet Me on the Oak Leaf"

Sunrise, sunsets, cloud shows, mirrored in park lagoons
wood chucks, deer, hawks, red fox, frogs, ducks, squirrels, geese and raccoons.
It gets icy in the winter and big puddles in the spring,
but all along it's beautiful and now you should help me sing.

Chorus:
Meet me on the Oak Leaf, meet me on the Oak Leaf.
You can run, you can shuffle, you can walk, you can roller blade
take a bike, take a break, you can just stand there.

Chorus:
Meet me on the Oak Leaf, meet me on the Oak Leaf
you can run, you can shuffle, you can walk, you can roller blade
take a bike, take a break, you can just stand there.
Meet me on the Oak Leaf, meet me on the Oak Leaf
meet me on the Oak Leaf, meet me on the Oak Leaf.

NOTES

Part I

1. Bobby Tanzilo, "Milwaukee Ruins: Pabst Whitefish Resort, Commerce Street & Stonehaven," *OnMilwaukee*, April 22, 2014, https://onmilwaukee.com/history/articles/mkeruins2.html.
2. "Foresight in '07…Fine Sight in '65," *Milwaukee*, August 1965, 30.
3. John Gurda, "Poetic Justice: It Takes a Visionary to Plant a Tree," *Journal Sentinel*, April 6, 2003.
4. Carl Swanson, "East Side Tunnel to Nowhere," *Milwaukee Notebook* (blog), December 4, 2017, https://milwaukeenotebook.com/2017/12/04/east-side-tunnel/. "In its November 26, 1940, issue, the *Milwaukee Journal* announced the donation. Included was a parcel between the river and the railroad tracks running from the tunnel north to East Edgewood Avenue. The 2,282-foot-long, eight-acre parcel varied between 150 to 258 feet wide. The newspaper said it was 'wholly unproductive property' but ideal for park purposes."
5. Jesse J. Gant and Nicholas J. Hoffman, *Wheel Fever: How Wisconsin Became a Great Bicycling State* (Madison: Wisconsin Historical Society Press, 2013), 2, 8.
6. Charlie House, "Bikes Booming," *Milwaukee Journal*, May 21, 1967.
7. Robert Penn, *It's All about the Bike: The Pursuit of Happiness on Two Wheels* (New York: Bloomsbury USA, 2010), 163.
8. Henry Norton, "Cycling to Nowhere," *Milwaukee Journal*, June 25, 1967, sec. 4, 1.

9. House, "Bikes Booming."
10. Andrew Ritchie, *Major Taylor: The Extraordinary Career of a Champion Bicycle Racer* (San Francisco/Mill Valley: Bicycle Books, 1988), 9. This book was later distributed in paperback by a different publisher. See also Taylor's autobiography, cited in Ritchie, 9.
11. Ibid., 79, 161, 91.
12. "Black Wheelman Was First to Cross the Tape Line," *Green Bay Press Gazette*, August 16, 1898.
13. House, "Bikes Booming."
14. John Gurda, "Charles Whitnall's Lasting Legacy for Milwaukee County," *Journal Sentinel*, September 1, 2017.
15. "Panther Hall of Fame: Harold 'Zip' Morgan," University of Wisconsin Milwaukee Panther Athletics, accessed April 29, 2018, http://mkepanthers.com/hof.aspx?hof=188&path=&kiosk=.
16. "1942 Victory Bicycle," Smithsonian Museum of American History, accessed January 8, 2018, http://americanhistory.si.edu/collections/search/object/nmah_1313316.
17. Mel Welsh, telephone interview with the author, December 17, 2017.
18. 1966 Milwaukee County Park Commission Report, 3.
19. "Lagniappe," *Milwaukee*, August 1965, 15. While much of this article is written in a witty or humorous style, the quote appears to be genuine.
20. Milwaukee County Board of Supervisors Proceedings, 74-43 Bike Trails, Applying for LAWCON/ORAP Funds (1974).
21. Milwaukee County Board of Supervisors Proceedings, 74-237 Bikeways, Accelerating Planning & Development (1974).
22. The Park People, "Milwaukee County Parks: A Short History," undated and unpaginated brochure.
23. "Bicycle History from the Late 19th Century," America on the Move, National Museum of American History, accessed January 29, 2018, http://amhistory.si.edu/onthemove/themes/story_69_3.html.
24. Milwaukee County Board of Supervisors Proceedings, 74-428, Bike Trails, Marking (1974).
25. Milwaukee County Board of Supervisors Proceedings, 64-682 (1964).
26. House, "Bikes Booming."
27. *Activities for All*, Milwaukee County Park Commission brochure, undated (but printed while Cornelius R. Dineen was president of the park commission, 1927–1955).
28. *Bicycling*, Milwaukee County Park Commission, March 1966, 1–2.
29. Ibid., 3–4.

30. Ibid., 6.
31. Ibid., 6–7.
32. Ibid., 18.
33. Ibid., 8.
34. Ibid., 12.
35. Penn, *It's All about the Bike*, 257.
36. Emily Van Dunk, Deborah A. Curtis, Jeffrey J. Brazzale, Anneliese M.Dickman, and Pooja Bhalla, "Public Spaces, Public Priorities An Analysis of Milwaukee County's Parks," Pulic Policy Forum, December 2002, 8.
37. Milwaukee County Board of Supervisors Proceedings, 77-1028, Marathon Race, Sponsoring (1977).
38. Milwaukee County Board of Supervisors Proceedings, 77-1028(a), Sponsoring Mini Marathon, 1979 (1978).
39. Milwaukee County Board of Supervisors Proceedings, 79-109, Lakefront Discovery Run, Holding (1979).
40. Milwaukee County Board of Supervisors Proceedings, 85-398, Runs, 5 mile+, Permits, Board Approval Required (1985).
41. Milwaukee County Board of Supervisors Proceedings (1989) (refer to the index at page 237).
42. Milwaukee County Board of Supervisors Proceedings, 73-972 Bike Riders Advisory Board, Creating (1974).
43. "About Us," Wheel & Sprocket, accessed July 28, 2018, https://www.wheelandsprocket.com/about/about-us-pg62.htm; "Inside Trek," Trek, accessed July 18, 2018, https://www.trekbikes.com/us/en_US/company/.
44. Milwaukee County Board of Supervisors Proceedings, 74-592, Bikeways, Coordinating with City (1974).
45. Milwaukee County Board of Supervisors Proceedings, 74-592, 76 Milwaukee County Bike Tour, developing (1975).
46. Milwaukee County Board of Supervisors Proceedings, 90-71 '76 Bike Trail/Tour, South Side Bike Trail Funds, Reprogrammed and Safety Lines, Installing (1990).
47. "Setting It Straight," *Milwaukee Journal*, May 4, 1976, 1.
48. Terry Devitt, "Bike Trail: 76 Mile Pleasure Path Waits for Fuller Use," *Milwaukee Journal*, April 27, 1976, 1.
49. Milwaukee County Board of Supervisors Proceedings, 86-198, '76 Bike Trail, Drexel Avenue Section, Construction of, Financial Assistance (1986).

50. Bruce Thompson, "Drexel Avenue Bike Path," *Wisconsin Bike Routes* (blog), May 5, 2013, http://www.wibikeroutes.net/blog/2013/05/drexel-avenue-bike-path/.
51. Milwaukee County Board of Supervisors Proceedings, 92-614, Ordinances, Bicycle Helmet Usage, Riders Age 14 & Under, Ordinance, Creating (1992).
52. Milwaukee County Board of Supervisors Proceedings, 73-210, Sheriff Patrolling Parks (1973).
53. Milwaukee County Board of Supervisors Proceedings, 73-210, Sheriff Patrolling Parks (1974).
54. Frederick M. Logan, "Lake Park Look-Back," *Let's See Milwaukee*, September 1964, 27.
55. Milwaukee County Board of Supervisors Proceedings, 79-939, Murder, Rape, Little Menomonee River Pkwy, Kletzsch Park, Reward (1979).
56. "Around the Town," *Milwaukee Journal*, August 25, 1979.
57. Milwaukee County Board of Supervisors Proceedings, 79-935, Lincoln Creek Parkway, Pedestrian and Bicycle Traffic, Hours (1979); Milwaukee County Board of Supervisors Proceedings, 78-1270, Root River Parkway Problems, Village of Greendale (1979).
58. "It's Time to Patrol Bike Trails," *Milwaukee Journal*, July 13, 1979.
59. Milwaukee County Board of Supervisors Proceedings, 82-850, Bicycle Trails, Safety/Security, Sheriff Patrolling, Budget (1982).
60. Milwaukee County Board of Supervisors Proceedings, 82-948, Bicycle Trails, Studying (1982).
61. Milwaukee County Board of Supervisors Proceedings, 82-948, Bicycle Trails, Studying (1983).
62. Milwaukee City Charter of Codes and Ordinances, "Bicycles and Snowmobiles," Vol. 1, Chapter 102, accessed February 18, 2018, https://city.milwaukee.gov/ImageLibrary/Groups/ccClerk/Ordinances/Volume-1/CH102.pdf.
63. "Crews Set to Work on Bicycle Path," *Milwaukee Journal*, July 27, 1984, sec. 2, 7.
64. Tom Held, "Police Arrest Suspect in Robbery on Oak Leaf Trail," *Journal Sentinel*, May 17, 2011, http://archive.jsonline.com/blogs/sports/122024163.html.
65. "History," United Performing Arts Fund, accessed May 1, 2018, https://upaf.org/what-is-upaf/mission/history/.
66. Milwaukee County Board of Supervisors Proceedings, 81-671, Arts Pedalers Bicycle Tour (1981).

67. United Performing Arts Fund, accessed June 18, 2018, https://upaf.org/upaf-events/.
68. Milwaukee County Department of Parks and Recreation, "Bucks for Bikes 1987," *Parkalendar*, September 1987.
69. "Milwaukee Lakefront Marathon," Badgerland Striders, accessed June 10, 2018, http://badgerlandstriders.org/events/milwaukee-lakefront-marathon-2/.
70. Milwaukee County Board of Supervisors Proceedings, 82-411, Parkways, Municipalities Assuming Responsibility for, Studying (1982).
71. Milwaukee County Board of Supervisors Proceedings, 82-948, Bicycle Trails, Studying (1982).
72. Milwaukee County Board of Supervisors Proceedings, 73-515, Noxious Weeds, Controlling (1973).
73. Milwaukee County Board of Supervisors Proceedings, 87-470, Dandelion Suppression Policy, Modifying (1987).
74. Milwaukee County Board of Supervisors Proceedings, 75-624(a), Bicycle Trails/Tours, '76 Bike Tour/Trail, Waukesha Bike Trail, Connecting to (1983).
75. *Milwaukee by Bike: 2011 Milwaukee Bicycle Map*, February 2011.
76. Milwaukee County Board of Supervisors Proceedings, 85-393, '76 Bike Tour Trail, Extending along Underwood Creek Parkway, Hold Harmless Agreements (1985); *Milwaukee by Bike: 2011 Milwaukee Bicycle Map*, February 2011.
77. Milwaukee County Board of Supervisors Proceedings, 86-56(a)(a), Bicycles/Bicycle Trails, East-West Segment, Establishing (1987).
78. Milwaukee County Board of Supervisors Proceedings, 85-315, Bicycle Trails/Tour, Root River Trail (1985). The resolution passed unanimously. The county executive stopped short of a veto and returned it unsigned, allowing it to remain in full force and effect.
79. Geoff Davidian, "Deputies Will Patrol Bike Paths," *Milwaukee Journal*, May 19, 1968; Milwaukee County Department of Parks, Recreation and Culture, *Your Milwaukee County 76 Bike Map*, May 1988.
80. Verne Scott, "History Project Essay 8," USA Triathlon, September 2011, https://www.teamusa.org/USA-Triathlon/About/Multisport/History/History-Project/Essay-8.
81. "The Ironman Story: Stepping into the Limelight," Ironman, accessed January 29, 2018, http://www.ironman.com/triathlon/history.aspx#axzz55apP83yE.
82. Arline M. Holliday, "Notes of the City of Milwaukee Bicycle and Pedestrian Task Force Meeting," June 9, 2008, 2.

83. Mayor's Bicycle Task Force, "Bicycle Milwaukee: Bicycle Plan for the City of Milwaukee, Wisconsin," ca. 1993, 3.
84. Milwaukee County Board of Supervisors Proceedings, 92-804, Bicycle Trails/'76 Bike Tour Bicycle Plan Preparation (1992).
85. Milwaukee County Board of Supervisors Proceedings, 93-794, Bike Trails, Budget 1994 (1993).
86. Milwaukee County Board of Supervisors Proceedings, 93-854, Bike Trails, Improvement, Upgrading Funding, Applications (1993).
87. "TEA-21—Transportation Equity Act for the 21st Century: Fact Sheet, Bicycle Transportation and Pedestrian Walkways," U.S. Department of Transportation, September 14, 1998, https://www.fhwa.dot.gov/tea21/factsheets/b-ped.htm.
88. Milwaukee County Board of Supervisors Proceedings 99-264, Parks, Recreation & Culture, Department of, Bicycle Trails East Side Bike Trail/Oak Leaf Trail Connecting Ramp, TEA-21 (1999).
89. Milwaukee County Board of Supervisors Proceedings 98-302(a)(a), Parks, Recreation & Culture, Department of, Bicycle Trails, North Shore Railway Conversion to Bikeway, WisDOT Agreement/TEA-21 Grant (1999).
90. "Milwaukee County Parks Development Grants 1993–2017," Milwaukee County Parks Department internal document.
91. "Bicycle Milwaukee: Bicycle Plan for the City of Milwaukee, Wisconsin," Mayor's Bicycle Task Force, ca. 1993, 1, Appendix B.
92. "2008 Annual Report," City of Milwaukee Bicycle and Pedestrian Task Force, 1.
93. Guy Smith, parks director, email with author, May 29, 2018.
94. Milwaukee County Board of Supervisors Proceedings, 98-14(a)(g) Easements, Bike Trail, City of Oak Creek, Stonewood Development Corp. (1998).
95. Milwaukee County Board of Supervisors Proceedings, 98-318, Easements, Bike Trail, Oak Creek Parkway, Wisconsin Electric Power Company (WEPCO) (1998).
96. Milwaukee County Board of Supervisors Proceedings, 98-320, Parks System, Bike Trails (1998).
97. Milwaukee County Board of Supervisors Proceedings, 95-380 (1995).
98. Milwaukee County Board of Supervisors Proceedings, 96-655, Easements, Henry Aaron State Park Trail, Veto, Sustained (1996).
99. "Bicycle Milwaukee: Bicycle Plan for the City of Milwaukee, Wisconsin," Mayor's Bicycle Task Force, ca. 1993, 13.

100. Lee Bergquist, "New Park in Menomonee Valley Will Be Named Three Bridges Park," *Journal Sentinel*, May 16, 2013, http://archive.jsonline.com/news/milwaukee/new-park-in-menomonee-valley-will-be-named-three-bridges-park-799vjg2-207794321.html.
101. Jay Walljasper, "Milwaukee's Home Run of Trails," *Rails-to-Trails*, Spring/Summer 2012, 10.
102. Tom Daykin, "Menomonee RiverWalk Will Have a Natural Feel, with Less Development—and Room for Bikes," *Milwaukee Journal Sentinel*, February 2, 2019.
103. "Coastal Management Grants," Wisconsin Department of Administration, 2018, https://doa.wi.gov/Pages/LocalGovtsGrants/CoastalGrants.aspx.
104. Jeramey Jannene, "Beerline Trail Open to the Public," *Urban Milwaukee*, October 14, 2010, https://urbanmilwaukee.com/2010/10/14/beerline-trail-open-to-the-public/.
105. Matt Lawrenz, personal correspondence with the author, October 13, 2018.
106. Harvey Botzman, *'Round Lake Michigan: A Bicyclist's Tour Guide*, 2nd ed. (Rochester, NY: Cyclotour Guide Books, 2002).
107. David Schlabowske, *Milwaukee By Bike Map*, Bicycle Federation of Wisconsin, June 2005.
108. Whitney Gould, "Parks Can Thrive, with a Little Help from Friends," *Journal Sentinel*, June 15, 2006, 6B.
109. Arline M. Holliday, "Notes of the City of Milwaukee Bicycle and Pedestrian Task Force Meeting," October 13, 2008, 1.
110. "Olympic Distance National Championships," USA Triathlon, accessed June 10, 2018, https://www.teamusa.org/USA-Triathlon/Events/USAT-Events-Calendar/2015/August/08/Olympic-Distance-National-Championships.
111. Steve Schultze, "Parks Need Tax Help, Report Says," *Journal Sentinel*, January 9, 2010, 1A.
112. *Park People News*, Summer 2012, http://parkpeoplemke.org/wp-content/uploads/2018/02/2012SummerNewsletter.pdf.
113. John Danielson, interview with the author, January 2018.
114. Laura Stark, "Wisconsin's Oak Leaf Trail," Rails-to-Trails Conservancy, December 5, 2017, https://www.railstotrails.org/trailblog/2017/december/05/wisconsin-s-oak-leaf-trail/.
115. Patricia Jursik, "The Oak Leaf Trail Deserves More Funding," *Bay View Compass*, July 2018, 3.

116. Southeastern Wisconsin Regional Planning Commission, "Non-Motorized Count Program Final Report," May 31, 2016, http://www.sewrpc.org/SEWRPCFiles/Transportation/Files/NMCounts/pilotprojecteport.pdf.
117. Tom Held, "Tour de Oak Leaf Trail," *Journal Sentinel*, July 7, 2008, http://archive.jsonline.com/blogs/lifestyle/31954704.html.
118. Arline M. Holliday, "Notes of the City of Milwaukee Bicycle and Pedestrian Task Force Meeting," Monday April 14, 2008, 2.
119. "Chris Kegel Awards & Accomplishments," Chris Kegel Foundation, accessed June 18, 2018, http://www.chriskegel.com/accolades-accomplishments/.
120. "Chris Kegel: The World's Most Generous Man," *Urban Milwaukee*, February 8, 2017, https://urbanmilwaukee.com/pressrelease/chris-kegel-the-worlds-most-generous-man/.
121. "Chris' Slow Roll," *Wisconsin Bike Fed*, June 2018, back page.
122. Tiffany Stoiber, "Construction Begins on Oak Leaf Trail Extension in Franklin," Journal Sentinel, August 10, 2017, https://www.jsonline.com/story/news/local/franklin/2017/08/10/construction-begins-oak-leaf-trail-extension-franklin/553930001/.
123. Dave Schlabowske, "Wisconsin Electric Assist Bicycle Laws," *Wisconsin Bike Fed*, June 2018, 19.
124. Wisconsin Administrative Code, Department of Natural Resources (NR), Chapters NR 1–99; Fish, Game and Enforcement, Forestry and Recreation, Chapter NR 45, https://docs.legis.wisconsin.gov/code/admin_code/nr/001/45/045.
125. Schlabowske, "Wisconsin Electric Assist Bicycle Laws."
126. Frank Berto, Ron Shepherd and Raymond Henry, *The Dancing Chain: History and Development of the Derailleur Bicycle* (San Francisco: Van der Plas Publications, 2000), 12.
127. Gant and Hoffman, *Wheel Fever*, 60.
128. "Bicycle Helmet," America on the Move, National Museum of American History, accessed January 29, 2018, http://amhistory.si.edu/onthemove/collection/object_176.html.
129. Dave Schlabowske, "Executive Director's Letter," *Wisconsin Bike Fed*, June 2018, 7. The author reports that Wheel & Sprocket sold fewer than thirty bikes at its 2017 expo and more than tripled that number the following year.

Part II

130. Charlie House, "Enraptured *Journal* Man Has Trail to Tell Bicyclists About," *Milwaukee Journal*, October 14, 1967, local news, women's, business and sports section, 1.
131. "Official Bicycle Trail Dedicated by County," *Milwaukee Journal*, October 15, 1967, sec. 2, 12.
132. "Milwaukee Bicyclist the Forgotten Man of Outdoor Recreation," *Milwaukee Journal*, October 19, 1967, sec. 1, 1.
133. Ritchie, *Major Taylor*, 61. At a Madison Square Garden race held years prior, riders did go off the edge of a banked track and flew into the crowd.
134. Jeff Drake and Jim Ochowicz, *Team 7-Eleven: How an Unsung Band of American Cyclists Took on the World—and Won* (Boulder: Velo Press, 2012), 55-60. Drake explains that executives pledged money toward building an Olympic velodrome to help host the Los Angeles games in 1984. Despite their sponsorship pledge, they could not initially envision what they were funding. A 7-Eleven executive famously asked, "What's a velodrome?"
135. Milwaukee County Board of Supervisors Proceedings, 80-670, Brown Deer Bicycle Track, Evaluating: Constructing Track of National Competitive Caliber (1980).
136. Heather Larson Poyner, "Works Began this Week to Fix Cracks in the Racing Track: Repairs Rolling at Veldrome," *Kenosha News*, October 12, 2016, http://www.kenoshanews.com/news/repairs-rolling-at-velodrome/article_b02e6a43-7368-596b-9022-6a2be86b759d.html; "About Us," Washington Park Velodrome, accessed March 9, 2018, http://www.kenoshavelodrome.com/about-the-kenosha-velodrome.
137. Milwaukee County Board of Supervisors Proceedings, 78-303 (a), Brown Deer Recreation Trail, Not Implementing (1979).
138. Increase Allan Lapham, *The Antiquities of Wisconsin, as Surveyed and Described* (Madison: University of Wisconsin Press, 2001), 19 and Plate VIII. He referred to the location as "Indian Prairie." He also noted an oak tree with an eight and a half foot circumference on this site in his 1850 survey.
139. Virginia Small, "Meet the Trailblazers behind Milwaukee's County Parks," *Milwaukee Magazine*, July 14, 2017, https://www.milwaukeemag.com/trailblazers-behind-milwaukee-countys-parks.
140. Friends of Kletzsch Park, accessed October 7, 2018, https://www.kletzschfriends.org/kletzsch-park-history.

141. Trevor Jensen, "David F. Schulz: 1949–2007," *Chicago Tribune*, October 10, 2007.
142. Laurie Muench Albano, "Recreation on the Milwaukee River," Milwaukee County, June 2002, http://county.milwaukee.gov/HistoryoftheParks16572.htm.
143. Milwaukee County Board of Supervisors Proceedings, 75-319, Bicycle Trails, Seeking Funds (1975).
144. Natalie Strohm, press release, Milwaukee County Percent for Art Program, May 3, 2010.
145. "Lincoln Park Golf Course," Milwaukee County Golf, accessed March 25, 2018, http://mke.golf/lincoln/.
146. Milwaukee County Board of Supervisors Proceedings. 79-935, Lincoln Creek Parkway, Pedestrian and Bicycle Traffic, Hours (1979).
147. Laurie Muench Albano, "Estabrook Park—Fact Sheet," Milwaukee County, March 1998, http://county.milwaukee.gov/HistoryoftheParks16572.htm.
148. Carl Swanson, *Lost Milwaukee* (Charleston, SC: The History Press, 2018), 170–72. Swanson's book includes interesting history and a colorful vignette of a 1942 Estabrook beach swimmer whose clothing was stolen, stranding him with only his swim trunks. He complained to an apathetic attendant and wrote a letter to the editor of the *Milwaukee Journal*.
149. Ibid., 172–73.
150. Terry Devitt, "Bike Trail: 76 Mile Pleasure Path Waits for Fuller Use," *Milwaukee Journal*, April 27, 1976.
151. John Swanson, "The Shorewood Apple Orchard Standoff," *Milwaukee Notebook* (blog), August 18, 2014, https://milwaukeenotebook.com/2014/08/18/shorewood-apple-orchard-standoff/#more-834.
152. Village of Shorewood, November 2, 2017, http://www.villageofshorewood.org/documentcenter/view/4689.
153. "Milwaukee County Landmarks: Shorewood," Milwaukee County Historical Society, accessed September 23, 2018, https://milwaukeehistory.net/education/county-landmarks/shorewood/.
154. Jay Walljasper, "Milwaukee's Home Run of Trails," 10.
155. Milwaukee County Trails Council documentation, "Oak Leaf Trail Eastside Summary," April 3, 2015, 1.
156. Carl Swanson, "A River Made for Recreation," Milwaukee Notebook, *Milwaukee Independent*, February 19, 2017, http://www.milwaukeeindependent.com/syndicated/milwaukee-notebook-a-river-made-for-recreation/.

157. Alex Vegelatos, "A Colorful, Controversial Corner: Shorewood's Southwest Sector," Shorewood Historical Society, accessed September 23, 2018, http://www.shorewoodhistory.org/southwest/index.html.
158. Danny Benson, "MKE in Wonderland: How an Amusement Park Created the Village of Shorewood," *MKE Memoirs* (blog), Milwaukee County Historical Society, July 23, 2013, https://milwaukeehistoryblog.wordpress.com/2013/07/23/mke-in-wonderland-how-an-amusement-park-led-to-the-village-of-shorewood/.
159. "Pedestrian & Bicycle Safety Committee," Village of Shorewood, accessed March 25, 2018, http://www.villageofshorewood.org/178/Pedestrian-Bicycle-Safety-Committee.
160. Laura Stark, "Wisconsin's Oak Leaf Trail."
161. Jeff Wagner, personal correspondence with the author, December 22, 2017.
162. Dolores Knopfelmacher and Gil Walter, *Lake Park Tree Walk* (Milwaukee: Lake Park Friends and Clark Graphics, 2003), 1.
163. Ibid., 16.
164. Carl Baehr, "Wahl Ave. Named After 'Grandfather' of Parks, *Urban Milwaukee*, September 2, 2016, https://urbanmilwaukee.com/2016/09/02/city-streets-wahl-ave-named-after-grandfather-of-parks/.
165. John Gurda, "Poetic Justice: It Takes a Visionary to Plant a Tree," *Journal Sentinel*, April 6, 2003.
166. Arthur P. Anello, *An Eclectic History of Milwaukee: A June 19, 1898 Street Car Ride Recreated* (Elm Grove, WI: Erickson & Rice. Ltd., 1983), 7.
167. "Submission to the National Register of Historic Places for Lake Park, Milwaukee, Wis.," sec. 7, 5.
168. "Photos: The End of the Line for Milwaukee's Lakefront Train Depot," *Milwaukee Journal Sentinel*, October 18, 2016, https://www.jsonline.com/picture-gallery/life/green-sheet/2016/10/18/photos-the-end-of-the-line-for-milwaukees-lakefront-train-depot/92315954/.
169. "Milwaukee History Timeline," Chudnow Museum of Yesteryear, accessed March 16, 2018, http://www.chudnowmuseum.org/milwaukee-history-timeline-1946-1979.html.
170. "Feasibility Report for South Lakefront Bikeway," Milwaukee County Park Commission, Division of Development, October 1972, 2.
171. "Full Cycle," *Milwaukee Magazine*, March 18, 2009, https://www.milwaukeemag.com/fullcycle/.
172. Dave Schlabowske, "Goodbye Otto Wenz, Jr., Wisconsin Cycling Superstar," Wisconsin Bike Fed, January 28, 2016, http://wisconsinbikefed.org/blog/2016/01/28/goodbye-otto-wenz-jr-wisconsin-cycling-superstar.

173. Milwaukee County Board of Supervisors Proceedings, 72-62, Cooperating with Milwaukee Wheelmen (1972).
174. Drake and Ochowicz, *Team 7-Eleven*, 30.
175. Milwaukee County Board of Supervisors Proceedings, 72-841, Bicycle Trail, Extend Lake Park Trail (1972).
176. Pete Zervakis, "Milwaukee County Weighs in on the Future of the Ravine Road Bridge," WTMJ 4, February 15, 2017, https://www.tmj4.com/news/local-news/ravine-road-bridge-future-milwaukee-lake-park-.
177. Milwaukee County Board of Supervisors Proceedings, 74-423, Bicycle Path, Cooperating with City (1974).
178. Milwaukee County Board of Supervisors Proceedings, 71-778a, Bicycle Path, Feasibility Report for Milwaukee River Bikeway (1972).
179. Milwaukee County Board of Supervisors Proceedings, 75-203, Lake Park Bicycle Trail, Extending (1975).
180. Terry Devitt, "Bike Trail: 76 Mile Pleasure Path Waits for Fuller Use," *Milwaukee Journal*, April 27, 1976, 1.
181. Milwaukee County Board of Supervisors Proceedings, 90-944(a)(a), Bikes/Bike Trails, '76 Bike Trail/Tour, Lake Park Trail, Lakeside Segment (North Ave. to Juneau Park Lagoon) (1991).
182. Milwaukee County Board of Supervisors Proceedings, 90-891, '76 Bike Trail/Tour, Chicago and Northwestern Segment, Lowenberg-Fitch Partnership (Landmark on the Lake Apartment Complex) (1990).
183. Milwaukee County Board of Supervisors Proceedings, 90-891(a)(a), Bikes/Bike Trails, '76 Bike Trail/Tour, Lake Park Trail, Lincoln Landmark Venture (Landmark on the Lake Apartment Complex) (1991).
184. "Final Designation Study Report: Coast Guard Station 1600 North Lincoln Memorial Drive," City of Milwaukee, August 2001, https://city.milwaukee.gov/ImageLibrary/Groups/cityHPC/DesignatedReports/vticnf/HDCoastGuard.pdf. As mentioned on page four of the report, well-known architect Alfred C. Clas designed a building for the site, but his plans were not used.
185. Bryan Rindfleisch, "American Indian Movement," *Encyclopedia of Milwaukee*, https://emke.uwm.edu/entry/american-indian-movement/.
186. "Coast Guard Station Milwaukee History," U.S. Coast Guard, Sector Lake Michigan, https://www.atlanticarea.uscg.mil/Our-Organization/District-9/Ninth-District-Units/Sector-Lake-Michigan/Units/Milwaukee/History/.
187. "Final Designation Study Report," City of Milwaukee.

188. Danny Benson, "Summerfest: Cold War Battleground," *MKE Memoirs* (blog), Milwaukee County Historical Society, July 7, 2013, https://milwaukeehistoryblog.wordpress.com/2013/07/07/summerfest-cold-war-battleground/.
189. Milwaukee County Board of Supervisors Proceedings, 72-363, Lake Park Nike (1972).
190. Olivia Barrow, "Bublr Bikes Seeks $5.5M for Future Bike Share Expansion," *Milwaukee Business Journal*, March 31, 2016, https://www.bizjournals.com/milwaukee/news/2016/03/31/bublr-bikes-seeks-5-5m-for-future-bike-share.html.
191. "MCTS+Bublr=Buslr," *Bublr*, January 16, 2018, https://bublrbikes.org/mcts-bublr-get-there/.
192. Milwaukee County Board of Supervisors Proceedings, 65-775 (1966).

Part III

193. Bill Felton, "The Loop Lives On," *Parks & Recreation*, October 1976, 18.
194. Anna Passante, "Tale of Our Tower," *Bay View Compass*, April 28, 2009, https://bayviewcompass.com/tale-of-our-tower/.
195. Anna Passante, "Up Periscope!" *Bay View Compass*, July 31, 2011, https://bayviewcompass.com/up-periscope/.
196. Jennifer London. "Landlubbers Need Not Apply," *Bay View Compass*, July 25, 2008, https://bayviewcompass.com/landlubbers-need-not-apply/.
197. "1975 Prize brochure," National Steel Bridge Alliance, Accessed February 1, 2018, https://www.aisc.org/globalassets/nsba/prize-bridge-brochures/1975prizebridgebrochure.pdf.
198. Milwaukee County Board of Supervisors Proceedings, 79-803, Hoan Bridge, Bicycle Lane" (1979).
199. Arline M. Holliday, "Notes of the City of Milwaukee Bicycle and Pedestrian Task Force Meeting," December 8, 2008, 2.
200. Patricia Jursik, "Guest Editorial: Bike and Pedestrian Path on Hoan," *Bay View Compass*, August 1, 2011, https://bayviewcompass.com/guest-editorial-bike-and-pedestrian-path-on-hoan/.
201. Marina Dimitrijevic, "WisDOT Public Meeting on Hoan Bridge Bike Path," *Marina's Message*, November 2011, http://county.milwaukee.gov/ImageLibrary/Groups/cntySupervisors/dimitrijevic/ENews/November20114thDistrictE-News.pdf.

202. Bruce Thompson, "New Bike Trail in Milwaukee," *Wisconsin Bike Routes* (blog), May 5, 2013. http://www.wibikeroutes.net/blog/page/2/. Thompson points out that this Kinnickinnic River Trail route was erroneously marked as completed on the Milwaukee County bike map for years prior to its opening.
203. "Fifth Choice" *Milwaukee Journal*, October 19, 1973.
204. Milwaukee County Board of Supervisors Proceedings, 77-981, South Shore Park, Constructing Recreational Facility (1977).
205. "Deep Tunnel," Milwaukee Metropolitan Sewerage District, accessed March 12, 2018, https://www.mmsd.com/what-we-do/wastewater-treatment/deep-tunnel.
206. Joe Peterangelo and Rob Henken, "Redevelopment in Milwaukee's Menomonee Valley: What Worked and Why?" Public Policy Forum, https://publicpolicyforum.org/sites/default/files/Valley%20report%20final.pdf, 49.
207. "Investigation of Elevated Bacteria Levels at South Shore Beach: *Escherichia coli* Source Detection Using Molecular-Based Methods," University of Wisconsin–Milwaukee Great Lakes WATER Institute technical report, June 2002, 1.
208. Keith Schubert, "New Planning and Design Study to Address Ongoing Water Quality Problems at South Shore Beach," *Bay View Compass*, August 1, 2017, https://bayviewcompass.com/new-planning-and-design-study-to-address-ongoing-water-quality-problems-at-south-shore-beach/.
209. "The Park People (TPP) Continues to Serve as a Conduit for Charitable Donations for our Parks," *Park People News*, Winter 2015, https://parkpeoplemke.org/wp-content/uploads/2018/02/2015Winterewsletter.pdf.
210. Jonathon Gregg, "Construction Project to Improve South Shore Park Will Impact Summer Events," Fox6 Now, June 20, 2017, http://fox6now.com/2017/06/20/construction-project-to-improve-south-shore-park-will-impact-summer-events/.
211. Don Behm, "Entire South Shore Park Beach to Be Moved to Avoid E. Coli and Frequent Closings," *Journal Sentinel*, September 14, 2018.
212. "Blue-Collar Beginnings," South Shore Yacht Club, accessed March 3, 2018, http://www.ssyc.org/club/our-history/our-origins; County Board of Supervisors Proceedings, 72-396, South Shore Yacht Club, (1972).
213. "Blue-Collar Beginnings," South Shore Yacht Club.
214. "Queen's Cup History" South Shore Yacht Club, accessed March 3, 2018, http://www.ssyc.org/queens-cup/qchistory.

215. Commodore Jerry Kedziora, "Membership Rolls Updated," South Shore Yacht Club newsletter, February 2018.
216. SS Milwaukee Clipper Preservation Inc., accessed April 3, 2018, http://www.milwaukeeclipper.com.
217. Charles B. Whitnall, "A Residential Park," 4. (This small blue brochure does not specify a date or publisher. It is available in the Charles Whitnall boxes at the Milwaukee County Historical Society.)
218. Jake Newborn, personal correspondence with the author, September 26, 2017.
219. Milwaukee County Board of Supervisors Proceedings, 70-72 Russell Ave. (1972).
220. Ron Winkler, *Bay View* (Charleston, SC: Arcadia Publishing, 2011), 118.
221. South Shore Frolics, accessed February 5, 2018, http://www.southshorefrolics.org/.
222. Milwaukee County Board of Supervisors Proceedings, 76-456, South Shore Park, Exchanging Land with Lauris & Dorothy Schuette (1976).
223. South Shore Park Watch, *Sneak Preview of the South Shore Bike Trail: A Segment of the Oak Leaf Trail*, October 2005, 3.
224. City of Milwaukee, "Pyro 02—Oak Leaf Trail South Shore," September 9, 2015, 1.
225. City of Milwaukee Bicycle and Pedestrian Task Force, annual report (2008), 3.
226. Anna M. Passante, *From Nojoshing to St. Francis, From Settlement to City: The Early History of St. Francis, Wisconsin, Part 1* (St. Francis, WI: St. Francis Historical Society, 2014), 3.
227. "Demolition Begins on Old St. Mary's Academy," WTMJ-Milwaukee, July 19, 2017, https://www.tmj4.com/news/local-news/demolition-begins-on-the-old-st-marys-academy; "Marian Center to Be Torn Down for Housing for the Nuns," WTMJ-Milwaukee, April 26, 2017, https://www.tmj4.com/news/local-news/marian-center-to-be-torn-down-for-housing-for-the-nuns.
228. Passante, *From Nojoshing to St. Francis*, 24. It is officially the Cardinal Muench Seminary Woods.
229. St. Francis Historical Society, "Lakeside Power Plant," sign erected 2018.
230. Milwaukee County Board of Supervisors Proceedings, 75-624, South Lake Front Bike Trail, (1975).
231. Felton, "The Loop Lives On," *Parks & Recreation*, 18.
232. Whitney Gould, "Development Breaks Up Shoreline Parks," *Milwaukee Journal Sentinel*, August 15, 1995, 1.

233. Dan Walker, "Stark Investments Closing Key Hedge Funds," *Journal Sentinel*, June 28, 2012, http://archive.jsonline.com/business/businesswatch/160680515.html?businessWatchDate=12-14-2016.
234. Tom Daykin, "Upscale St. Francis Lakefront Apartments Get First OK," *Milwaukee Journal Sentinel*, September 26, 2018, https://www.jsonline.com/story/money/real-estate/commercial/2018/09/26/large-st-francis-lakefront-apartment-plan-gets-first-city-approval/1430530002/.
235. Passante, *From Nojoshing to St. Francis*, 5.
236. "Milwaukee County Landmarks: Cudahy," Milwaukee County Historical Society, accessed March 5, 2018, https://milwaukeehistory.net/education/county-landmarks/cudahy/.
237. Rebecca Roepke and Michelle Gibbs, *Sheridan Park: A Centennial History of Cudahy's First Park 1914–2014* (Cudahy, WI: Friends of Cudahy Library, 2014), 9.
238. Ibid., 8, 28.
239. Ibid., 7.
240. Ibid., 15.
241. "Milwaukee County Landmarks: Cudahy," Milwaukee County Historical Society.
242. Milwaukee County Park Commission, Division of Development, "Feasibility Report for South Lakefront Bikeway," October 1972, 3.
243. Milwaukee County Board of Supervisors Proceedings, 72-671, S Side Lakefront (1972).
244. Roepke and Gibbs, *Sheridan Park*, 31.
245. "Warnimont Bluff Fens (No. 352)," Wisconsin Department of Natural Resources, accessed March 1, 2018, https://dnr.wi.gov/topic/Lands/naturalareas/index.asp?SNA=352.
246. Milwaukee County Board of Supervisors Proceedings, 68-476, Cudahy Gun Club (1968).
247. Jesse Garza, "Milwaukee County to End Lease with Cudahy Sportsmen's Club," *Milwaukee Journal Sentinel*, November 6, 2014, http://archive.jsonline.com/news/milwaukee/milwaukee-county-to-end-lease-with-cudahy-sportsmens-club-b99386251z1-281859751.html/.
248. "Air Defense Command in Area Reorganized," *Milwaukee Journal*, August 24, 1961.
249. Tom Brandstetter, personal email with the author, September 10, 2015.
250. County Board of Supervisors Proceedings, 72-1065(a), Senior Citizen Complex, Using "Nike" Site in Warnimont Park (1973).

251. Laurie Muench Albano, "History of the Parks: Grant," Milwaukee County, accessed March 1, 2018, http://county.milwaukee.gov/HistoryoftheParks16572.htm.
252. Avery Wittenberger, *Milwaukee County Parks on Parade* (Milwaukee: Milwaukee Journal, 1965), 20.
253. Ibid., 20.
254. Nels Monson and Dean S. Marlow Jr., *South Milwaukee* (Charleston, SC: Arcadia Publishing, 2004), 97.
255. "Experience an Exceptional Lifestyle: History," North Shore Country Club, accessed January 15, 2018, http://www.nscountryclub.org/history.
256 "Milwaukee County Parks: Grant Park," Milwaukee County, updated April 2018, https://county.milwaukee.gov/files/county/parks-department/Park-Maps/grant.pdf.
257. Bill Kurtz, "History Takes Its Course in Grant Park," *Milwaukee Journal*, February 29, 1988, 3b.
258. Milwaukee County Board of Supervisors Proceedings, 74-792, Bike Trail, Creating in Oak Creek" (1974).
259. Jeff Baudry, "Big 2015 for Grant Park," Milwaukee County, January 12, 2015, http://county.milwaukee.gov/ImageLibrary/Groups/cntyParks/media/2015-Press-Releases/011415_GrantParkUpgrades.pdf.
260. South Milwaukee Yacht Club membership director Karen "Kiki" Kilman, personal email with the author, March 4, 2018; "Club History," South Milwaukee Yacht Club, accessed March 1, 2018, http://www.smyc.net/History.aspx.

INDEX

B

Badgerland Striders 29, 40, 50, 68
Bay View Park 32, 117, 118, 120, 121, 122
bicentennial 43
Brown Deer Park 28, 35, 79, 80
Bublr 101, 102

C

Chicago and Northwestern Railroad 82, 93
Civilian Conservation Corps (CCC) 81, 104, 126
Coast Guard 98, 99, 106
Cudahy Gun Club 127, 128
Cudahy, Patrick 20, 122, 132
Cupertino Park 106, 110

D

Department of Natural Resources 30, 57, 58, 61, 66, 74, 97, 104, 111

E

Elroy-Sparta State Trail 37
Estabrook Park 9, 33, 35, 36, 37, 38, 80, 82, 83, 84, 85, 96

F

ferry 112, 113

G

Ghost Train 87
Grant Park 20, 30, 33, 35, 36, 37, 44, 45, 46, 50, 69, 97, 113, 121, 122, 124, 127, 128, 129, 130, 131, 132, 133, 134

H

Hank Aaron State Trail 48, 60, 61, 62, 63, 64, 69
Hoan Bridge 49, 50, 56, 60, 106, 107, 108

I

Intermodal Surface Transportation Efficiency Act (ISTEA) 56, 57

INDEX

K

Kegel, Chris 10, 71, 72
Kletzsch Park 47, 80, 81, 84

L

Lake Park 32, 47, 90, 92, 96, 97, 100, 104, 130
Land and Water Conservation Fund (LAWCON) 30
Lincoln Park 50, 81, 82, 96

M

marathon 21, 39, 51, 55, 67, 88
McKinley Park 96, 98, 99
Milwaukee 64 26, 32, 107, 120
Milwaukee 76 26, 29, 30, 33, 43, 45, 51, 105, 109, 114, 124, 132

N

1972 U.S. Road Racing Championships 95
Nojoshing Trail 121

O

Oak Leaf Trail 9, 10, 11, 16, 17, 18, 25, 26, 29, 32, 33, 37, 38, 51, 58, 59, 64, 65, 66, 67, 68, 71, 72, 74, 75, 77, 82, 84, 85, 87, 89, 91, 92, 99, 101, 103, 104, 106, 107, 110, 112, 113, 114, 117, 119, 121, 122, 123, 124, 126, 127, 128, 129, 132, 133, 134, 135
Olmsted, Frederick Law 20, 90

R

railroad right-of-way 37, 38, 80, 85, 87, 89, 93, 107
rails-to-trails 37, 62, 74, 89

S

security concerns 46
Seminary Woods 120, 121
Sheridan Park 36, 69, 70, 122, 123, 124, 126, 134
signs 32, 33, 43, 45, 48, 54, 59, 65, 78, 83, 96, 97, 110, 111, 114, 121, 127
South Shore Park 30, 110, 111, 113, 114, 116, 117, 121, 126
Stano, John 72, 137

T

Taylor, Marshall 23, 24
Trails Council 66, 72
Transportation Equity Act for the Twenty-First Century (TEA-21) 58

U

UPAF Ride for the Arts 37, 49
Urban Ecology Center 62, 77, 89

V

velodrome 37, 79
Veterans Park 51, 90, 94, 99
Victory bicycles 76

W

Warnimont Park 69, 100, 127, 128, 129, 130, 134
Wheel & Sprocket 10, 37, 41, 71
Whitnall, Charles 19, 20, 24, 25, 34, 113, 131, 134
Whitnall Park 10, 25, 45, 50
Wisconsin Electric Power Company 36, 51, 59, 79, 103, 120

ABOUT THE AUTHOR

Burton Davis.

Jill Rothenbueler Maher grew up jogging, biking and cross-country skiing with her family in southeast Wisconsin. After moving to Washington, D.C., she enjoyed the Washington & Old Dominion Trail and logged countless hours training for duathlon races. Back in Milwaukee, she enjoys sunrise runs and Saturday rides with friends on the Oak Leaf Trail. She regularly writes for the *Bay View Compass* and has degrees from the University of Minnesota and Georgetown University. *Milwaukee County's Oak Leaf Trail: A History* is her first book.

Visit us at
www.historypress.com